On the
Social and Emotional Lives of Gifted Children

Issues and Factors in Their Psychological Development

SECOND EDITION

On the
Social and
Emotional
Lives of
Gifted
Children

Issues and Factors
in Their Psychological
Development

SECOND EDITION

Tracy L. Cross

PRUFROCK PRESS, INC.

ISBN 1-59363-002-6

At the time of this book's publication, all facts and figures cited are the most current available. All telephone numbers, addresses, and Web site URLs are accurate and active. All publications, organizations, Web sites, and other resources exist as described in the book, and all have been verified. The authors and Prufrock Press, Inc., make no warranty or guarantee concerning the infor-mation and materials given out by organizations or content found at Web sites, and we are not responsible for any changes that occur after this book's publica-tion. If you find an error, please contact Prufrock Press, Inc. We strongly rec-ommend to parents, teachers, and other adults that you monitor children's use of the Internet.

Prufrock Press, Inc.
P.O. Box 8813
Waco, Texas 76714-8813
(800) 998-2208
Fax (800) 240-0333
http://www.prufrock.com

For Ben

To my favorite unsung heroes,

Eva Ruth Cross
and
Jennifer Cross

Table of Contents

Gifted Children Today   85

Where We Have Been and Where We Are Going   125

Foreword

On the Social and Emotional Lives of Gifted Children lives up to its title. The book presents in a highly readable style observations on the psychology of giftedness, the education of gifted children, and the state of our knowledge about child development. Tracy Cross obviously listens to parents and children. Using his knowledge of the field, as well as his experience as a psychologist, administrator, and parent, he fashioned a series of columns in Gifted Child Today that are reproduced in this book. He avoids introducing jargon that is only understood by the in-group and puts the complex ideas in a readable, accessible form. Important concepts are introduced and explained. Readers will find no panaceas here, but rather reasoned, thoughtful commentaries on helping children to reach their potential. Those looking for a quick fix will have bought the wrong book, yet readers will find sound advice on a variety of topics. Academics who choose this book for one of their courses will find the blend of research and practical ideas engaging and thought-provoking for their students.

Tracy Cross' personality comes through in the text. One encounters a consistency of caring and a sensitivity to the dangers of generalization when we are speaking of human beings. His ideas are not static and locked into the way it is supposed to be. Rather, he is responsive to acute societal changes, as seen in pieces that refer to horrific events like September 11 and Columbine, as well as slower, relentless forces such as the Internet that are altering adult-child relationships. A persistent theme is his assertion that one cannot speak of giftedness without paying attention to context. The manifestation of giftedness in various talent domains does not happen accidentally. Many supporting and distorting factors interact for giftedness to emerge. This book offers a healthy and balanced perspective on the social and emotional lives of children who are gifted and talented.

—Laurence J. Coleman

Preface

I have always been a psychologist and aspiring philosopher. As a young child, I often pondered the nature of people—why some had to starve while others wasted resources, why some made friends so easily and others seemed to be left out, how it was possible that some incredibly nice, warm, and caring people could also be racists. Psyche had me from an early age. These same issues in one form or another still dominate my thinking today.

My best friend from age 3, Rick Allen, had an older brother named Ron whom I could tell did not quite fit in with others. While my friends occasionally made fun of him for being "different," the adults seemed to be both intrigued and entertained by him. I often watched him out of the corner of my eye, fascinated by this extraordinary young mind. He truly aspired to be President, but first he needed to go to Yale. Tall order for a 6-year-old! While my friends and I practiced football, Ron was creating plans for his ascent to the Presidency. Ron did graduate from Yale University Law School, and he did become president, not of the United States, but rather of the International Young Trial Lawyers Association. Ron died in an unfortunate swimming accident at age 44. He lived a productive and meaningful life working on behalf of others. This book is in the memory of Ron and the Allen family, one of the earliest and most important influences in my choosing this career path.

Other key events drew me into the field of gifted studies. As a teenager, I came to realize how bright my mother was. I also came to understand how the circumstances in her life—having grown up on a farm and graduated from a small rural high school as valedictorian at age 15—led her down a path of unrealized potential. An early marriage, four children in 6 years, and the typical sacrifices made by her generation of adults destined her to live her short 48 years as an unsung hero. The times and circumstances in which my mother grew up clearly limited her opportunities in life. This book is also dedicated to her memory. Since the first edition of this book, I am happy to report that, through funding from the Jacob Javits and Advanced Placement Incentive programs, the Indiana Academy for Science, Mathematics, and Humanities is bringing academic opportunities for high-ability students from modest backgrounds living in small rural communities. Students from 14 schools throughout Indiana are benefiting from Project Aspire.

As a teenager, I had the fortune of working at my family's art gallery. I studied the artists who spent untold hours at the gallery interacting with Knoxville's "old money" and "nouveau riche." I learned from this experience that some extraordinarily talented people struggle to live by certain societal rules. I watched as several of these artists/professors at the local university self-destructed. I learned that society's expectations can be brutal reminders of the consequences of being gifted, but nonconforming.

My wife and I met while in high school. I became close to her gifted siblings—five children identified as academically gifted in one family. I studied them for years as I became a young man. Their vast differences were an early lesson for me about the diversity of people with gifts or talents.

In graduate school, I met Laurence J. Coleman (Larry). We worked together evaluating the Tennessee Governor's School Program and studied students' experiences of being gifted. Over the past 20 years, Larry and I have focused on the lives of gifted students in various types of settings and locations. We have produced numerous articles, chapters, and one textbook entitled *Being Gifted in School: An Introduction to Development, Guidance, and Teaching*. Larry's guidance and inspiration have been invaluable to me in my professional development.

While on faculty at the University of Wyoming, I made a lifelong friend in Roger Stewart. For 4 years, he and I burnt the midnight oil together working on numerous studies. Roger is a brilliant mind who does more to help other people than anyone I have met. He is a scholar and a gentleman. His influence on me is great.

This book was inspired by all these important people who taught me many life lessons. The actual idea for creating this book, however, came from Sally Reis, who encouraged me to compile the columns I had written for *Gifted Child Today* (*GCT*) into a book. I am thankful to Sally for her kind words that lead me to pursue this endeavor.

The text for this book was written over the past 9 years. The material, with one exception, is made up of the regular columns I wrote for *GCT*. The exception is an invited piece for *GCT* wherein a number of professionals in the field were asked to contribute our top 10 list of important events influencing the field of gifted education over the past century.

The book begins with an introductory chapter. The chapters have been organized into four themes: "About Gifted Children: Who They Are and Why," "Guiding Gifted Children," "Gifted Children Today," and "Where We Have Been and Where We Are Going." In total, there are 21 chapters on the social and emotional development of gifted students and the description of important events that have occurred over the past 100 years. Each of the chapters includes key concepts at the beginning and discussion questions at the end. The book concludes with a list of references and a Resources section that includes a comprehensive list of contact information for parents, counselors, and teachers across North America. I hope this book provides ideas that are helpful in understanding the social and emotional development of gifted students and how teachers, counselors, and parents can work together to guide their development.

Several people worked very hard to complete this edition of the book. I would like to thank Jennifer Cross for helping me during the project by editing, proofreading, and providing advice throughout the process. She also helped me during the original writing phase of the columns that appeared in *GCT*. I would like to thank Jim Kendrick for carrying out all the important editorial work to bring this project to fruition. I also want to thank Joel McIntosh for supporting many of my efforts over the past 12 years. Judy Margison was instrumental in gathering the materials for the Resources section and providing assistance and wisdom throughout the revision process. I also want to thank Roy Weaver, dean of Teachers College at Ball State University, for his support for more than a decade. And, a final note of thanks go to my children, Ian, Keenan, Colin, and Eva, for reminding me on a daily basis of the importance of advocating for gifted students and the joy of being a parent.

Introduction:
A Continuum
of Psychological Services

Key Concepts

- Continuum of Psychological Services
- Personal and professional biases

The social and emotional development of gifted students involves many issues and considerations. Those who have written on the subject during the past 25 years or so have tended to support the following claims: Gifted students have social and emotional needs; gifted students' needs are often unique to them; there are specific characteristics of gifted students; and those characteristics create or reflect needs. A much smaller group of authors have claimed that gifted students tend to experience life much the same as their nongifted peers; their social and emotional needs are often determined by the qualities of the environment in which they find themselves; and there are few, if any, characteristics that are identical across gifted students. Some areas of agreement have been that gifted children are, in fact, children first; that early experiences in life are important as they develop; and that adults have important roles to play in the social and emotional development of gifted students. Over the past 10 years, authors have encouraged the field to focus more attention on the nongeneral developmental patterns of students with gifts or talents and the different contexts in which gifted students exist (e.g., Coleman and Cross, 2001).

Growing interest has been seen in gifted students who manifest extraordinarily high IQ scores. These students have been called "profoundly," "severely," and "exceptionally" gifted. While limited data exists on those students, much of which is anecdotal from clinicians who provide therapeutic services to one or more of them, the nature and needs of this group of gifted students have not been fully documented.

To help provide a framework for understanding the ideas in this book, I have created a Continuum of Psychological Services that illustrates the wide range of needs gifted students have and the potential role that differing groups of adults need to help them play. The Continuum of Psychological Services (Cross, 2001) also makes evident that parents, teachers, and counselors need to work together to cover most of the services gifted students will need and that no one person can play all the roles needed.

Continuum of Psychological Services

In this Continuum of Psychological Services, advising is the broadest need area. This includes general life advice, such as how to choose a tie, or more specific information, such as what courses to consider taking. Because of the broad range of activities and the level of expertise needed to carry them out, many individuals will be capable of providing this service to gifted children.

The guidance position is slightly more focused than advising in that it tends to deal mostly with academic or school-related matters. These can vary significantly from course selection to relationship building. Teachers are often key in providing guidance to students on a daily basis. Guidance counselors provide this service to a few students and generally with a higher level of professional preparation.

The counseling position requires more specific training in counseling theories and techniques than the previous two positions. This category overlaps with both advising and therapy. I see it as different in that it naturally tends to revolve around school-based matters and there is always a large built-in clientele for a school counselor or social worker.

The fourth position of therapy is broader than counseling in the sense that it can pertain to almost any presenting problem. How I see it differently than counseling is that therapy can take years to complete, is typically done outside schools, and often involves seeing a therapist in a private setting. Therapy often also deals with much more serious or dangerous problems than does school counseling. I have placed the counseling and therapy headings in these two places on the continuum because, in many situations, counseling is primarily educative and therapy ameliorative. In essence, then, the continuum moves from general advice to trying to remedy behavioral problems via medication.

The final position on the continuum is that of psychopharmacology. I use this term because of the current pattern in our culture of parents seeking medical treatments for behavioral problems. This pattern often yields some form of drug therapy along with counseling-based treatments. Psychiatrists and family physicians are typically the professionals who deliver this type of service. However, referrals from school psychologists, school counselors, and social workers can also lead to the labels that are often treated with medications. A common pattern, however, is a direct referral from a parent to the family physician.

While I recognize that my Continuum of Psychological Services is rather elementary and clearly one could argue for different interpretations of the roles of each group and the overlap across services, the value of the Continuum is that it illustrates the need for collaboration across groups of people. For example, if a parent has a concern about a child, quite possibly the child's teacher and others have some important information to share. Without efforts of collaboration, the parent can only hold one perspective of the child. This need for collaboration guarantees that multiple perspectives in differing settings can be included in a discussion. The Continuum also establishes a model of whom to pursue first based on the kind of issue or concern that exists.

The next four sections of the book are a reflection of my thinking about the lives of gifted students. I have tried to make clear when I am reporting on research or when I am offering my own opinion. These writings reflect my personal and professional predispositions. The first is the eclectic nature I bring to the study of this phenomenon. To that end, I use psychological, educational, sociological, and anthropological data. I also draw on 20-plus years of serving gifted students in a variety of roles, including researcher, teacher, counselor, psychologist, administrator, and parent.

The last section of the book, Resources, is new for this edition. It provides information to teachers, counselors, and parents that enable them to get their questions answered in a local manner. The resources provided represent the kinds of information that address the several thousand questions I have been asked over the past quarter-century. The information is also provided in an attempt to encourage the creation of networks of those interested in gifted children within states and across North America.

A bias I have is that I believe that all people live in differing subcultures that are very much impacted by the time in history in which they happen to grow up. Consequently, the study of gifted students necessarily must take these factors into consideration.

A second bias I have is that I believe people are influenced by their own sense of human agency. And, while genetic predispositions clearly exist and are important, I believe that the developing person is able to change over time in ways that reflect an interaction with their environment. Consequently, the context in which gifted people live impacts their psychological development.

Another bias that influences my thinking is that I believe theories are just that—theories—educated social constructions subject to evolution over time with additional information and in differing contexts. I believe that the construct of giftedness necessarily must be considered in light of societal values and with an awareness of dominant subgroups. In an effort to transcend these biases, I try to seek many forms of data. I see skepticism as an important part of the interpretation of any theory or "statement of fact." I encourage all readers to develop a healthy sense of skepticism—not cynicism, but an ability to question what others may accept as fact.

This book represents my perspective on the social and emotional development of gifted children, colored by my training, experience, and beliefs.

For Discussion

- What is the value of the Continuum of Psychological Services?

- Academic- and school-related matters are mentioned as topics that would be addressed by individuals in a guidance position. Name issues/matters related to gifted students that might be addressed in other positions on the Continuum of Psychological Services.

- Reflect on and discuss the biases you may bring to the study of gifted children.

About Gifted Children: Who They Are and Why

This section contains eight chapters, all of which focus on a description of the gifted child. In my first column for *Gifted Child Today*, "Examining Beliefs About the Gifted," I felt it was important to present some information about myself and how I have come to believe what I have about gifted children. The primary thrust of this chapter is that I do believe that there is such an entity as a gifted child and that we should be cautious not to impose one dominant perspective on our efforts to identify the social and emotional needs of this widely diverse group.

In "Determining the Needs of Gifted Children," I discuss the difficulty in determining the social and emotional needs or "issues" that are unique to gifted children. This is not an easy task because so much of what we believe on the matter has been determined before the completion of substantial research. In subsequent chapters, I discuss many other factors that gifted children experience. In "Competing With Myths About the Social and Emotional Development of Gifted Students," I examine several of the myths about giftedness that are commonly held by parents, teachers, and administrators, as well as by gifted students. Challenging these myths is the first step in lessening the potentially negative effects on gifted students' social and emotional development.

Understanding a gifted child's development is also facilitated by examining psychological theory. Thus, in the fourth chapter, "Gifted Children and Erikson's Theory of Psychosocial Development," I overview Erik Erikson's eight stages of psychosocial development and relate them to the development of gifted children. I emphasize the need for adults to interpret a gifted child's behaviors in light of both Erikson's theory and a gifted child's idiosyncratic development and personal characteristics.

For years while interacting with gifted children, their parents, and their teachers, ideas about who gifted children are and what makes them different from others troubled me. I was finally able to draw many of these ideas together in a column titled "A Consideration of Axiomatic Statements." These statements offer in a nutshell many of the principles that underlie my beliefs about guiding gifted children. The notion that gifted children are children and people just like everyone else is an important one to remember for those who work with them. The exceptionalities we see are not the *only* aspect of a child's development and may not even be the most significant one. These axiomatic statements provide a strong foundation for an understanding of the mixed messages gifted students receive on a daily basis.

"How Gifted Students Cope With Mixed Messages" takes a look at some of the research Larry Coleman and I have done into how gifted students deal with the expectations society places on them.

My research into the suicides of three students associated with a residential high school for gifted students led me to publish two columns on this very important and serious topic. The first of these, "Examining Claims About Gifted Children and Suicide," is placed in this section because of its emphasis on gifted adolescents who have committed suicide and how difficult it is to know more about these troubled children. It also attempts to provide guidance to adults about what can and should be done to avoid suicidal behavior of gifted students.

The final chapter, "On Chance and Being Gifted," examines the role of psychobiological, cultural, sociohistorical, and family influences on the lives of gifted children.

This group of chapters will set the stage for an understanding of who gifted students are, and I hope they will give you pause as you examine your beliefs about them.

Examining Beliefs About the Gifted

When I first began writing a regular column for *Gifted Child Today* addressing salient issues pertaining to the social and emotional needs of gifted students, I felt it most appropriate to outline how I hoped to develop the column over time. My first step was to introduce myself in an effort to provide the readership enough information to make an informed decision about whether or not to read the column. This is important information for readers of this book, as well.

I hold a doctoral degree in educational psychology from the University of Tennessee–Knoxville. My original training was very quantitative in nature. Later, however, I took additional coursework and also apprenticed for 3 years under the tutelage of a phenomenologist. I have been a college professor at a land-grant university, two state universities, and a small liberal arts college and have studied gifted students throughout the nation. For the past 4 years, I have served as the executive director for a state-funded residential school for academically gifted adolescents. Even though I realize that this information is far more interesting to me than it is to you, I am quite sure that each of these facts has influenced my views of the world. So, *caveat emptor*!

In the *GCT* columns and in this book, I tried to provide information and ideas that would pique the interest of some, prompt hallway conversations among some, and, perhaps, raise the dander of others. To that end, my approach varies from offering basic factual information to arguing points through syllogism, to reporting on studies I have conducted. I try to present at least two major lines of thought on important topics and often try to situate the focus of each chapter within the research base, while at the same time elucidating concerns about how we have come to hold certain beliefs. To reach these goals, I tried to write the columns that have been adapted into this book in a style that would be as accessible to as large an audience as possible.

Clarifying Beliefs About the Gifted

The topic of discussion, the social and emotional needs of gifted students, presupposes some important beliefs. Some of those include that gifted people do exist; they are identifiable, we have established a process to identify them, and, consequently, we have identified them (at least enough of them to educate our biases); those we have identified represent the real thing; and once we have identified them, we can make reasonable decisions about what their social and emotional needs are.

Unless I am wrong about this rather elementary syllogism, any broken link might cast doubt on the general topic of debate, or at least limit what is knowable about the topic. In this first column, I will discuss a few of these assumptions.

Is there evidence that gifted people do exist? At this point, I feel quite comfortable in claiming that most educators would acknowledge that some people manifest extraordinary abilities. We have heard of or personally know people who seem to read markedly better, run faster, jump higher, do high-level mathematics before they can talk, paint remarkable works of art, or play the piano masterfully at an early age. In short, human variation stares us in the face every day of our lives. Hence, gifted people do seem to exist.

There are at least two approaches we use to come to grips with the manifest differences across people. The first is to conclude that people who do not demonstrate the exceptional qualities previously listed are less than adequate, while the second approach is to label the aforementioned people as exceptional and call them *gifted*. I like the second option better myself. As reasonable as this logic may seem on the surface, the decision to establish nongifted folks as normal has some important intellectual baggage. For example, when I think of the term *needs* (as in social and emotional needs of the gifted), I reflect upon my upbringing when my parents would attempt to teach me a lesson. The lesson usually began with a statement like "Tracy, you need to . . . " I remember thinking, "According to you, I may need to, but to me I am okay with the way I am currently doing it."

In short, by establishing the gifted as different, we become normal, thus elevating ourselves into the position of deciding what the needs of gifted people are.

The term *needs* is considered by some as a direct reflection of the values of a dominant group in society. Moreover, much of the research conducted on this topic has been done over the past 60 years. During this time, many groups of people (e.g., Native Americans, African Americans, Hispanic Americans) have been conspicuously missing from the ranks of the identified gifted. Therefore, we should be aware of the historical context and the absence of voice reflected in many of the studies seeking to shed light on the needs of gifted children.

Defining Terms

A final point is that one of the difficult aspects of being considerate when trying to understand the needs of gifted students is that social and emotional needs may not be static. That is to say, the environment in which one exists may greatly impact these needs, or the mere definition of need has to be contextualized.

In short, at this point in history we can say that serious consideration must be given to the terminology used to describe gifted students and its relationship to cultural power, the voices that are missing from the dialogue, and the relative influence or determination of environmental factors on the nature of the needs of the gifted. Food for thought.

So, as we continue this dialogue, I assert that it would be prudent to constantly remind ourselves to question from whose perspective we are establishing and defining the nature of the social and emotional needs of gifted students.

For Discussion

- Reflect on and discuss how the inclusion of North American minority groups (e.g., Native Americans, African Americans, Hispanic Americans) in gifted education research may change prevailing beliefs.

- Discuss how the environment may impact the needs of a gifted individual.

Determining the Needs of Gifted Children

Key Concepts

- Buescher's developmental framework
- Social and emotional needs/issues of gifted versus nongifted children
- Cultural influences on gifted children

This chapter will pick up where the first one left off by posing two questions frequently asked about gifted students: Do gifted students really have social and emotional needs and, if they have these needs, are they the same as their nongifted peers?

For years, researchers, clinicians, and educators have tried to untangle the complicated relationships among the general ability, family dynamics, specific culture, and school experiences of children in order to build models of the social and emotional development of gifted children. From the myriad studies cutting across the psychological paradigms and the concomitant research techniques employed, I feel it has been established that children do develop emotionally and socially and, consequently, do have needs or, perhaps more appropriately stated, issues in these areas. An important contribution to the research base was by Thomas Buescher (1985) in an article entitled "A Framework for

Understanding the Social and Emotional Development of Gifted and Talented Students." In this article, he outlined a developmental framework to be used for identifying social and emotional concerns of gifted students. The framework includes six "Dynamic Issues of Giftedness During Adolescence":

Ownership:	Who says I am gifted anyhow?
Dissonance:	Recurrent tension between my performance and my own expectations.
Risk-Taking:	Should I be taking new risks or seeking secure situations?
Others'	
Expectations:	Being pushed by others' expectations, being pulled by my own needs.
Impatience:	I have to know the answer right now!
Identity:	What counts is who I am. (p. 14)

This framework allows us to identify possible needs of gifted children based upon the qualities and issues relevant to the individual child, rather than trying to create an omnibus list of needs for all gifted children. This is an important point and will be discussed as part of the response to the second question.

Now, on to the question about whether the social and emotional needs of gifted children are different from those of their nongifted peers. There are two lines of thought on this question. The traditional consideration is that differences need to be ferreted out if they exist, which suggests the importance of distinctions being made across needs between gifted and nongifted children. The alternative consideration is that it really matters not whether the differences exist as long as the phenomenon of what gifted children's social and emotional needs are has been captured and depicted. In short, focus on what is for gifted children without regard for their nongifted peers. One of the reasons this debate is important is that the two research positions often lead to differing research approaches being taken. In turn, the approaches define what is knowable about the social and emotional needs of gifted children. And, like viewing the world through an eye patch on either the right or left eye, one's perception of reality is always attenuated by the view.

I believe that there is not sufficient evidence in the research lore to unequivocally claim that gifted children have social and emotional needs that are qualitatively different from or mutually exclusive of their nongifted peers. Having said this, I will discuss two issues that I think are critical to my position. The first was noted previously: the search for omnibus needs that cut across all gifted children is misguided. The second is that the differences in needs are likely a function of the relationship of the individual child's talents and his or her social interactions within the prominent communities of his or her world (e.g. family and school).

In the politics of research exploration, there is a desire to build a model or list of needs that encompasses all children. This goal fuels and is fueled by the common wisdom, myths, and speculation about what gifted children's needs might be. In my opinion, not enough consideration has been given to other qualities and experiences the gifted child has that would influence his or her needs. For example, lists abound of the nature and needs and the characteristics of gifted children. These lists include claims that are always wide ranging and often inconsistent. And, at the same time, we have all known students who fit some or much of the information not on the list. To rectify this situation, I recommend we redefine the concern from that of need by using the term Buescher and others have used: *issue*. The question would change to "What are the social and emotional issues of gifted children?"

As the research base on the social and emotional development of gifted children grows, along with the evolving research approaches being taken, a clear message is emerging. That is, the culture in which a child is immersed has an important influence on the experience of being gifted. The cultural values interact with the social goals of the student and the issues associated with growing up in America. Therefore, the social and emotional needs of any particular gifted child may be predictable, but cannot be decided a priori. In short, although the characteristics of the gifted child, along with certain environmental factors, might create conditions where needs should exist, unless the individual child perceives or experiences the needs, they do not exist—no matter what a list might include or expert might say.

So what can we say? Where can we turn for reasonable information? I suggest that, if you are interested in reviewing some of the salient research on the topic that reflects these two lines of thought, you should consider the following authors. Dr. Linda K. Silverman is a leader in the field who has written a textbook on counseling the gifted in which she discusses her beliefs about what the social and emotional needs are and how to address them from a clinician's perspective. Laurence J. Coleman represents an alternative line of thinking that can be reviewed in his 1985 textbook, *Schooling the Gifted* (Addison-Wesley), and in miscellaneous articles (e.g., "Is Being Gifted a Social Handicap?" [1988], which I co-authored). Coleman emphasizes the influence the relationship between the environment of a school and the gifted child's desire to feel accepted in the environment has on his or her social and emotional needs. Both Silverman and Coleman are fine researchers who provide worthwhile perspectives on the social and emotional needs of gifted children.

For Discussion

- How would you respond to an individual who asserts that research into the social and emotional needs of gifted children should focus on determining how their needs differ from nongifted children?

- Discuss the idea that immersion in a particular culture has an impact or influence on the experience of being gifted.

Competing With Myths About the Social and Emotional Development of Gifted Students

Key Concepts

- Myths about giftedness have negative effects on the social and emotional development of gifted students
- Myth 1: Gifted students should be with students their own age.
- Myth 2: Gifted students should be in same-age heterogeneous classes.
- Myth 3: Gifted students should be perfectly well-rounded.
- Myth 4: Being gifted is something you are just born with.
- Myth 5: Everyone is an expert in giftedness.
- Myth 6: Adults know what gifted students experience.
- Myth 7: Being too smart in school is a problem, especially for girls.
- Myth 8: All kids are gifted/no kids are gifted.

As a person who has dedicated himself to the study of the psychological and experiential lives of gifted students, I have encountered several widely held myths and associated practices that have negative effects on the social and emotional development of gifted students. These myths are common among parents, teachers, administrators, and gifted students. As a wise person (Lao Tsu) once said, "Nothing is more difficult than competing with a myth." Doing so, however, can create tremendous opportunities for people. Recall that it was not that long ago that myth prevented women from competing in long distance foot races.

The following list includes some of the most common and insidious examples of myths pertaining to the social development of gifted students. I hope that by discussing these examples, gifted students will be better served and barriers to their well-beings will be broken.

Myth 1. *Gifted students should be with students their own age.* The worry expressed here is that something inappropriate or untoward will occur if different age groups spend time together. Parents, teachers, and administrators worry that groups of multi-age children will struggle with exploitation, intimidation, inappropriate modeling, and sexuality. This prevailing myth undergirds some advocates' preferences for educational models that emphasize enrichment rather than acceleration. The logic is as follows: "We should keep the students together even if they have already mastered the material." Some believers of this myth will claim that research supports this point, but in fact they are mistaken. Writers have published this sentiment, but research does not support this idea. In fact, in my research with Larry Coleman, it is clear that gifted students need opportunities to be together with their intellectual peers, no matter what their age differences (Coleman & Cross, 2001). While there are plenty of appropriate reasons to provide enriching educational experiences, these decisions should not be made out of fear, worry, or myth; they should be based on the needs of the students.

Myth 2. *Gifted students are better off if they spend their entire school day amidst same-age, heterogeneous classmates.* The claim is that if we allow gifted students to be clustered together through one of any means available, they will be unable to get along with others later in life, and this experience will cause emotional distress. Middle school principals and some middle school teachers regularly expressed these feelings. This concern includes the belief on the parts of the adults that gifted students, to be happy, must become socially astute. Becoming socially astute requires that gifted students spend as much time as possible in heterogeneous classroom environments. Once again, the claimed research that supports this myth is virtually nonexistent. Imagine all the opportunities students have to interact with other people. Church, sports, clubs, meals, camps, are just a few examples. Sacrificing learning and creating frustration based on this myth is unethical, in my opinion. This problem increases as the students develop and their knowledge base increases within a specific discipline.

Myth 3. *Being perfectly well-rounded should be the primary goal for gifted student development.* Please note the carefully chosen phrase, "perfectly well-rounded," as opposed to "somewhat well-rounded." Many parents, teachers, and administrators believe that it is their role to ensure that gifted students are perfectly well-rounded. To that end, they will encourage, prod, goad, push, threaten, and yell at gifted students to get them to spend less time engaged in their passion areas, so they can engage in something the adult wishes them to do. A very common example is that of an introverted gifted student who has great facility with computers. Adults will drag the child away from her passion to get her to participate in something she may loathe. While adults in each of these roles should be concerned with the well-being of gifted students, requiring them to engage in activities for which the gifted student has no interest (e.g., going outside and playing, or spending time with other children you do not choose to play with during the school day) as a means to make them happy later in life is misguided. Much of the research on successful gifted adults has revealed that they spent considerable amounts of time, often alone, in their passion areas as children. A more reasonable approach is to encourage and nurture other interests in the child rather than sending them the message that they are unacceptable as they are. For example, sending gifted children to a residential summer program can do wonders to broaden interests within a community where they feel emotionally safe and accepted for who they are.

Myth 4. *Being gifted is something with which you are just born.* A corollary to this is that things come easily when you are gifted or being gifted means never having to study or to try hard in school. This naïve notion of giftedness, while intuitively proper, can be debilitating to gifted students' development. Many teachers, parents, administrators, and gifted students hold this belief. It is not informed, however, by research on talent development and development in general. Moving from an *entity* notion of giftedness to an *incremental* notion, wherein talent is developed with hard work and some failure, is a much healthier and more nurturing experience of being a gifted student (Dweck, 1986).

This change in understanding of giftedness is of particular importance before age 10 or so. That is because a school's curriculum tends to get more focused as it moves toward middle school. Many gifted students experience this change as personal failure, causing self-doubt and distress, because they have internalized intellectual struggle as failure. To change this belief merely requires teaching gifted students about the two definitions, exposing them to models who failed in the process of great accomplishment (e.g., Thomas Edison) and having them go through processes that include struggle as part of growth.

Myth 5. *Virtually everybody in the field of gifted education is an expert on the social and emotional development of gifted students.* An extension of this is that every adult (parent, teacher, school administrator) is an expert on the social and emotional development of gifted students. The field of gifted studies is quite small, often yielding professionals in the field who are called on to be experts in numerous areas. This regularly plays out with a high percentage claiming expertise and being called on to provide wisdom on this topic. Another reason for this situation is the fact that we were all students once ourselves and that, supposedly, makes us familiar with gifted students' lives. This is similar to my having played football as a youngster and now claiming expertise equivalent to that of Peyton Manning. Many factors combine to create situations where competing advice—sometimes by people who mean well, but do not know the research on the social and emotional development of gifted students—is given. As the field of gifted studies grows and matures, I think that children would be better served by having the expertise of those who specialize, rather than relying on a model that requires its experts to know a little about everything associated with the field.

Myth 6. *Adults (parents, teachers, and administrators) know what gifted students experience.* This plays out on issues such as being around bullies and drugs, sexuality, and social pressures. In addition to the usual generational differences, in many ways, contemporary experiences are different from the experiences of previous generations. For example, many gifted students go to school fearful of schools as unsafe environments. Gifted students of today are often surrounded by guns, and when not, still perceive that they are. In short, the vague red menace of previous generations has been replaced by generalized anxiety and fear; fear that the media has exacerbated and kept alive in ways that are inescapable by today's youth. The hubris of adults to believe that they know what gifted students experience on a daily basis is mind-boggling. Consider these two facts: the suicide rate of adolescents rose more than 240% between 1955 and 1990, and suicide is the second leading cause of death of this age group (Holinger, Offer, Barter & Bell, 1994). Is it possible that our children live in a somewhat different context than adults did at the same age? If parents can observe classrooms more often, talk with their gifted children, asking for descriptions of their experiences, then a much richer understanding is possible.

Myth 7. *Being too smart in school is a problem, especially for girls.* This myth has many facets to it. It represents adults' worries about their own feelings of acceptance; concerns about fears associated with standing out; the typical anti-intellectual culture of schools; the reflection of society's under evaluation of high levels of achievement; and the often mentioned, intuitively based association of high levels of intellectual ability with low levels of morality. The obvious consequence of this myth is the nurturing of incredibly high percentages of our students who underachieve in school. A large proportion of American students with gifts and talents have developed social coping strategies that use up time, energy, limit their opportunities, cause bad decisions to be made, retard their learning, and threaten their lives. These behaviors and beliefs about self make perfect sense when one perceives the mixed messages about being gifted in their school's social milieu. We must provide support for these children as they navigate the anti-intellectual contexts in which they spend much of their time.

Myth 8. *All kids are gifted, and no kids are gifted.* This myth is most often expressed by administrators and occasionally by teachers. The reasons for these two beliefs are predictable given the developmental differences that manifest across the grade levels. For example, while in the elementary grades, which are thought to have a more amorphous curriculum than the later grades, teachers typically perceive manifestations of potential for extraordinary work as indicators of giftedness. As the child moves toward high school where the curriculum tends to be quite focused, with distinct disciplines being taught by teachers passionate about the subject areas they teach (we hope), giftedness is often determined as meaningful only as a manifestation of success within the specific courses. Middle school represents some of both of these operative definitions of giftedness.

Another important aspect to this belief is the primary motivator that led teachers and administrators to pursue their profession. For example, when you ask elementary teacher candidates what they want to do most, they will tell you that they want to teach young children. Secondary teachers tend to say that they want to teach math, English, and so forth. Middle school teachers often hold very strong views about the specific age group of students with whom they have chosen to work. These teachers and administrators often describe the primary school-based needs of middle school students in terms of social needs and their need to learn in a protective environment that emphasizes the students' developmental frailties. A rigorous educational curriculum is seldom the highest priority.

Another undercurrent to these positions is that being gifted is tied to the assumption that gifted children are better than other students. This is a very unfortunate connection, because it encourages adults to hold the position that all kids are gifted or no kids are gifted. James Gallagher, a wise man in the field of gifted education, once said "When someone claims that all kids are gifted, merely ask them 'In what?'" Being gifted eventually has to be in something. While all kids are great, terrific, valuable, and depending on your beliefs perhaps even a gift from God, they are not all gifted in the way the term is used in the field. Giftedness is not an anointment of value. A person who shows extraordinary ability for high levels of performance when young and, if provided appropriate opportunities, demonstrates a development of talent that exceeds normal levels of performance, is gifted.

I hope that providing a list of some of the pervasive and insidious myths that affect the lives of gifted students will inspire us to take action on behalf of the students. If we challenge these myths with examples of good research, provide appropriate counseling and create learning environments where students with gifts and talents can thrive, then many of these myths can be eliminated. Let us work to help all students have an appropriate education, including gifted students.

For Discussion

- A number of myths about gifted students and giftedness are discussed. Discuss instances when you (as a teacher, parent, or counselor) taught, guided, or counseled a gifted child based on information that you now know is a myth. How would you handle a similar situation now?

- Based on the myths discussed, how would you (as a teacher, parent, or counselor) change your practices?

Gifted Children and Erikson's Theory of Psychosocial Development

Key Concepts

- Erikson's theory of psychosocial development has eight developmental stages.
- Psychosocial development is facilitated by resolving crises.
- Erikson's view of the development of one's identity is important in the overall development of people.

In this chapter, I will provide an introduction to one of the most influential thinkers in the field of psychology, Erik Erikson. After I overview his theory of psychosocial development, I will tie it to the development of gifted children. Erikson was a young contemporary of Sigmund Freud, the father of psychoanalysis. Erikson discussed growing up in Europe with one biological parent being Jewish and the other Gentile. He described himself as being a tall, blonde-haired, blue-eyed person with a big nose. He said that people in the Jewish community called him "the goy" (non-Jew), while those in the Gentile community called him "the Jew" (Erikson, 1972).

As he grew, he came to feel that he had experienced a crisis of identity. After studying children, Erikson forwarded a theory of psychosocial development. His theory had as its core the notion of developmental stages through which a crisis must be resolved. His theory was important for many reasons. It established a framework for understanding the typical psychosocial developmental patterns of people. It broke with traditional thinking of psychologists of the period, which held that people cease developing after adolescence. Erikson's theory claimed that people continue to develop across their lifespan. Another important feature of Erikson's theory was that it postulated that a person's id is free from internal conflict but susceptible in its development to psychosocial conflict, not internal psychosexual conflict as Freud had claimed. Erikson meant that conflict arises not from the internal forces of the person, but rather the person's interaction with his or her environment. Indeed, culture is important to a person's development. This position was undoubtedly influenced by Erikson's interactions with Margaret Mead.

Erikson defined eight developmental stages during which a crisis must be resolved in order for a person to develop psychosocially without carrying forward issues tied to the previous crisis. During the *infancy stage* (the first year-of-life), he proposed that the primary crisis to be resolved is one of trust versus mistrust. Erikson labeled the task to be resolved during the second year-of-life (*toddler stage*) as autonomy versus shame and doubt; the *preschooler stage* (years 3–5), as initiative versus guilt; and the *elementary school stage*, competence versus inferiority. As the children move into *adolescence*, he or she must refine his or her sense of identity versus role confusion; in *young adulthood*, intimacy versus isolation; in *middle adulthood*, generativity versus despair; and in *older age*, integrity versus despair. According to Erikson, as the individual negotiates a crisis at each stage of development, basic strengths or virtues emerge. The following are the eight basic virtues that Erikson believed emerged across psychosocial development: hope, will, purpose, competence, fidelity, love, care, and wisdom, respectively.

I have come to believe that Erikson's view of the development of one's identity is very important in the overall development of people. I also have come to believe that the previous and subsequent stages of development (1–4 and 6–8) are influenced by this drive to establish an identity. In tying this to the lives of gifted students, I will focus on the stages (1–5) of typical school-age children.

As parents, teachers, and counselors, we are often the significant adult figures in the lives of gifted children. To guide their psychosocial development, we should pay great attention to the crises Erikson described as occurring during the first 18 years of life. For example, during the *infancy stage*, parents are the primary care givers who see that the basic needs of the child are met. Food, shelter, and proactive efforts at comforting the infant lead it to hold a basic trust about the world. When children's needs are not met at this critical early stage, an imbalance of mistrust results and sets the stage for a basic mistrust of the environment and those in it.

As children continue to grow and become *toddlers*, they grapple with issues of autonomy. If encouraged to explore age-appropriate and accomplishable tasks, they will develop a heightened sense of autonomy. In Western society, a common term used to describe children of this age is "the terrible twos." While it is quite clear that the increase in physical movement and experimentation is physiologically based, as parents of children in this age group, we often experience their behavior as terrible. This experience on the part of the parents can lead them to discourage their children's explorations of their world. If discouraged, or if children explore with no regard for age-appropriate tasks, they will develop self-doubt and shame. Once again, imagine how people's lives differ if they operate from a strong sense of autonomy or self-doubt and shame.

Between the ages of 3–5 (the *preschooler stage*), children attempt to find the balance between striking out on their own (initiative) and fearing to do so (guilt). As adults, it is important to encourage early efforts at self-initiating behavior. For example, if young children indicate a willingness to pursue activities, either independent of their parents or just beyond their previous successes, parents need to encourage the behavior. If children do not learn it is acceptable or advisable for them to initiate activities on their own, then they learn to feel guilty. It is sad to see a five-year-old child who manifests a heightened sense of guilt.

Identification of giftedness is often linked to early evidence of ability. The potential success of any identification process to locate children of extraordinary ability is often subject to the extent to which children have developed a sense of autonomy and engage in self-initiating behaviors. According to Erikson, not successfully resolving the crises of the previous three states will have a negative impact on later life. In addition, the culmination of not resolving the crises will reduce the likelihood of children being identified as gifted.

During the *elementary school stage* of Erikson's theory, ages 6–12, the child's psychosocial crisis is competence versus inferiority. Clearly, teachers, counselors, and parents all have a stake in and the possibility of positively affecting the child's development during this stage. It is important that the group of adults work together to see that gifted students have ample opportunities to successfully complete meaningful work. This should not be limited to in-school activities. The meaningful nature of the work is crucial, but unfortunately often missing from what adults expect or tolerate in gifted children's lives. Adults should anticipate several successful efforts on the part of the child before the child's internal assessment of being competent will be affected. As the child successfully completes tasks, the adults need to provide variation in both task and location of the activities.

According to Erikson, during *adolescence*, a primary aspect of developing one's identity deals with role confusion. Puberty disrupts the predictability and understandings an individual has developed as a child, and the search for identity is the paramount psychosocial experience for the adolescent. Often, cliques form and manifest exclusionary behavior. Everyone who passed through adolescence was affected to some extent by this search for identity. This "over identification" with a desired group is actually "a defense against a sense of identity confusion" (Erikson, 1972, p. 262). Adolescents search for who they are. Their determination is made by attempting to integrate what they believed themselves to be as children, their newly discovered libidos, and their vision of their future selves. Erikson stated that the adolescent mind is essentially a mind of the moratorium—a psychosocial stage between childhood and adulthood (i.e., the morality learned by the child and the ethics to be developed by the adult). It is an ideological mind. Indeed, it is the ideological outlook of a society that speaks most clearly to the adolescent who is eager to be affirmed by his peers and is ready to be confirmed by rituals, creeds, and programs which at the same time define what is evil, uncanny, and inimical (Erikson, pp. 262–263).

Gifted adolescents develop a sense of self through various interactions with groups of people. Erikson called this trying on different hats. He believed that becoming a healthy adult is necessarily tied to resolving the crisis of identity or suffering the feelings associated with role confusion.

Resolving this crisis successfully is complicated in Western cultures given the mixed messages that society sends to gifted students. The messages can be so confusing that gifted students will engage in numerous behaviors to cope (Coleman & Cross, 2001). Some approaches include hiding or pretending to be what one is not. Other coping approaches include underachievement or other behaviors with potentially serious consequences.

Guiding the development of gifted children requires adults to work together in seeing that the children successfully resolve the crises that Erikson outlined in the eight stages of psychosocial development. Parents, teachers, and counselors should be aware that an individual gifted child may be affected by the psychosocial crisis at earlier ages than Erikson believed. Adults should realize that some gifted children have an intellectual ability to understand the world years ahead of their chronological age but have the emotional development typical of their same-age peers. To take full advantage of the explanatory power of Erikson's theory, one needs to interpret an individual gifted child's behaviors in light of the theory and the child's idiosyncratic development and personal characteristics. Armed with this information, adults are well prepared to help guide the psychological development of gifted children.

If Erikson was right that successful resolution of the psychosocial crises he outlined will result in gifted children leading their lives with feelings of hope, will, purpose, competence, fidelity, love, care, and wisdom, imagine what good can spring from well-adjusted proactive gifted adults.

For Discussion

- Reflecting on Erikson's theory of psychosocial development and the asynchronous development of gifted children, describe behaviors of gifted children that may be explained by this theory.

- The importance of adults working to see that gifted students have ample opportunities to complete meaningful work successfully is noted. Discuss how you can provide such opportunities for the gifted children in your family or school.

A Consideration
of Axiomatic Statements

Key Concepts

- Gifted and nongifted individuals share developmental characteristics.
- Gifted individuals have unique life experiences.
- Gifted individuals are impacted by external influences.

In this chapter, I would like to remind teachers, parents, and counselors of some of the most important influences on the psychological development of gifted students. With an awareness of these influences, adults can more effectively guide and nurture the development of these children in the social and emotional realms.

I hope to clarify these concepts with axiomatic statements that illustrate many of the salient considerations across the life of a gifted student. Perhaps this will help you think of the ways in which gifted students are the same as others, different from others, and how they are impacted by outside influences.

- *Gifted students share many developmental characteristics and problems with all people.*

Gifted students are children first; as such, they have much in common with children of average ability.

People develop over time; as people, gifted students develop over time.

Because talents manifest in numerous domains, children remain a very heterogeneous group of people; as children, few to no claims would be equally true for the entire group of gifted students.

Every child grows up in a different environment; as children, gifted students grow up in different environments.

People are agents in their own lives; as people, gifted students are agents in their own lives.

Children vary in a multitude of personal characteristics; as children, gifted students vary in a multitude of personal characteristics.

People need to feel accepted; as people, gifted students need to feel accepted.

Knowledge is largely believed to be a construction of the person. As a subset of one's knowledge base, social cognition is developed idiosyncratically through the eyes of an immature mind.

Influencing the perceptions a person has about his or her life that were formed at an early age is often a difficult endeavor; as people, it is also difficult to influence the perceptions formed early in the lives of gifted students.

Influences on the belief systems and behaviors of children begin with parents, continue with family members, but often are transcended by peer influence as the children get older, with the potential of significant others influencing them as they mature; as children, the same pattern is true for gifted students.

A person's development is idiosyncratic; hence, patterns of development for gifted students will probably not closely reflect developmental milestones that are derived by averaging across groups of people.

Environmental influences on a child can never transcend biologically based potential; as children, this is true for gifted students, as well.

- *Gifted students have life experiences and issues that are different just because they are gifted.*

Because they have extraordinary capabilities, gifted students will likely experience certain aspects of the world differently from those who do not share the same gifts or talents.

Giftedness is often experienced as feeling different from other students and, unlike other exceptionalities, can be hidden. Consequently, gifted students as agents in their own lives behave in compliance with their survival needs and social goals.

- *Influences outside the individual have an impact on gifted students.*

Groups of people in society are treated differently relative to opportunities, expectations, and stereotypes; as people, gifted students' experiences will be affected by variables they cannot control.

Definitions of giftedness change over time and vary in different societies. Whether or not children are thought to be gifted, how they are treated, and what subsequent perceptions and behaviors they engage in are variable and likely to be culturally relevant.

Americans maintain numerous views of gifted students simultaneously. Gifted students receive mixed messages about their places in society, and that is often interpreted to be an indicator of the degree to which they are accepted and can be themselves.

Schools tend to acknowledge and reward achievement over time (hence, labels such as *overachiever* are often given to gifted students to account for this prejudice for averaging achievement). Students of outstanding ability may be overlooked if their achievement is not consistently manifest (if gifted students manifest enough extraordinary work to be noticed, but not enough to satisfy others, they are labeled *underachiever*).

As gifted students get older, a primary task they have to complete in their psychological development is identity formation. Considering the axioms provided, one could argue that the various, simultaneous, and often contradictory messages gifted students receive during their lives, when screened through perceptions that were developed when they were very young, destine gifted students to engage in numerous patterns of social coping behavior. These observed patterns may appear unreasonable or naïve to adults who have not experienced the world in the manner in which gifted students do. The challenge that teachers, parents, and counselors of gifted students must meet is to create learning environments in which gifted students feel fully accepted and that are, at the same time, sophisticated in their approaches to developing the students' talents.

For Discussion

- Name and discuss some of the mixed messages that gifted individuals receive.
- Are the mixed messages the same for gifted girls and gifted boys?
- How does the nature of these messages change over the life span?

How Gifted
Students Cope
With Mixed
Messages

Key Concepts

- Stigma of Giftedness Paradigm
- Continuum of Visibility

In the previous chapter entitled "A Consideration of Axiomatic Statements," I provided an overview of three categories of statements about the lives of gifted students. The first category was entitled "Gifted students share many developmental characteristics and problems with all people." It portrayed ways in which gifted children are like other children. The second category of axiomatic statements was called "Gifted students have life experiences and issues that are different just because they are gifted." This set of statements attempted to characterize some specific differences in experiences that gifted students have as compared to their nongifted peers. In the final set of statements, "Influences outside the individual have an impact on gifted students," I tried to illustrate how others' beliefs about giftedness potentially affect gifted students. The three sets of statements portrayed the lives of gifted students as existing within a world that sends them mixed messages that convey numerous unfavorable notions of the meaning of giftedness.

In this chapter, I am continuing the effort to illustrate how gifted students deal with these mixed messages. More specifically, I will relate what Larry Coleman and I have found to be a reasonable description of the experience of giftedness and how these students cope with life. From our research, we have posited that, for many gifted students, a figural aspect of the experience of giftedness is that of being stigmatized. Over the past 15 years, our research has shown time and again that this is an important component of the experience. In his book *Schooling the Gifted* (1985), Larry proposed a "Stigma of Giftedness Paradigm" that has three parts:

1. gifted students want to have normal social interactions;
2. they believe that others will treat them differently if they learn of their giftedness; and
3. gifted students learn that they can manage information about themselves in ways that enable them to maintain greater social latitude.

Patterns of Gifted Students' Coping Behaviors

Given this set of beliefs, gifted students become active agents in trying to establish for themselves, against the backdrop of mixed messages, a degree and type of social latitude and experience that minimizes pain while allowing them to deal with the issues that change as they develop. Many of their strategies are rather obvious, while others are tacit knowledge for them. The combined set of strategies was originally characterized on a Continuum of Visibility with Total Visibility (playing a stereotypic role associated with being gifted in order to stand out from others) on one end, Blending In (finding ways to avoid standing out from the larger group of students) in the middle, and Disidentifying (proactively engaging in behavior that one believes is associated with a subculture's stereotypes that is opposite the group of which the gifted child might naturally be a part) at the other end.

Continuum of Visibility

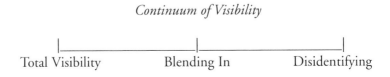

| Total Visibility | Blending In | Disidentifying |

For example, one student may choose to play the role of mad scientist to stand out as much as possible from others, while another chooses to navigate school along gender-typed expectations by sublimating academic interests with what they perceive as more acceptable behaviors, such as dating or competing in athletics. Other types of coping behaviors include underachieving in school and more serious efforts like suicide. Typically, however, the coping behaviors of gifted students tend to be less harmful, sometimes evolving into behaviors that have some benefit to their academic performance, such as studying more and reading to escape. Depending upon one's social goals, the behaviors of gifted students tend to fall into the categories listed on the continuum. With the exception of the Total Visibility category, the others reflect the students' desire to manage information. Consequently, their behaviors to that end are situation-specific; for example, not responding in school when a teacher asks a question (Blending In), or making friends with cliques of children in school whose reputation would be opposite that of gifted students (Disidentifying; e.g., becoming a "doper" instead of a "nerd").

My more recent research has caused me to add to the continuum a fourth position that reflects the most dire efforts at coping: taking one's own life. It fits the continuum notion in that the behaviors are coping efforts. It is different, however, in view of the fact that I am unsure of the extent to which the coping is more connected with managing giftedness and its interrelatedness with larger life issues, or merely an act most closely associated with depression and other correlates of suicide. We must concern ourselves, however, with the broader issue of the conditions in which gifted students live and what we as adults (teachers, counselors, parents) do to assist their development and what we may unknowingly do to send them mixed messages. I believe that we need to take stock of our own beliefs about gifted students and seek additional training to prepare ourselves to assist in the development of all students.

The lives of gifted students are both the same as and quite different from other students' lives. Understanding the pain and suffering that children experience is only the beginning of what we as the nurturers of gifted students need to know. To minimize the mixed messages gifted students perceive, teachers, counselors, and parents must communicate expectations and beliefs held about giftedness. When they are congruent, the messages the students perceive will be more similar, thus allowing them to thrive. When the messages are dissimilar, gifted students will engage in numerous coping behaviors, many of which are detrimental to their development and success as students. If you would like to read in greater detail about the lives of gifted students from Larry's and my perspective, then I encourage you to read any of the references listed below.

Coleman, L. J. (1985). *Schooling the gifted.* New York: Addison Wesley.

Coleman, L. J., & Cross, T. L. (1988). Is being gifted a social handicap? *Journal for the Education of the Gifted, 11*, 41–56.

Cross, T. L., Coleman, L. J., & Terhaar-Yonkers, M. (1991). The social cognition of gifted adolescents in schools: Managing the stigma of giftedness. *Journal for the Education of the Gifted, 15*, 44–55.

For Discussion

- Name and discuss some of the mixed messages that gifted individuals receive.

- Are the mixed messages the same for gifted girls and gifted boys?

- How does the nature of these messages change over the life span?

- Reflect on an incident (as a teacher, counselor, parent) in which you unintentionally sent a mixed message to a gifted child. How would you handle a similar situation differently?

- What steps can you (as a teacher, counselor, parent) take to ensure that a gifted child does not engage in strategies that result in him or her "blending in" or becoming "invisible."

Examining Claims About Gifted Children and Suicide

Key Concepts

- Risk factors for adolescent suicide
- Paucity of research on gifted adolescent suicide

This chapter deals with a very sobering topic, one that appears too often in the newspapers, elicits strong opinions, and strikes fear in the hearts of parents: the suicides of gifted adolescents. In the following pages, I will provide an overview of what can and cannot be said on the topic based on actual research. I will focus my comments on gifted adolescents, even though preadolescents have died by their own hand. I will limit my comments to adolescents since they constitute by far the greater percentage of suicides (as compared to preteens) and since there is more information available on this age group. Please note the term *information*, rather than *data*. This distinction foreshadows the paucity of research on the topic that will be discussed.

One characteristic of our culture is the growing rate of its population that commits suicide. Increases over the past decade are seen in virtually every age group, with the 15–24 age range showing significant increases. Suicide ranks as the second leading cause of death among young people (Capuzzi & Golden, 1988). One should note that adults older than 70 years have shown large increases in their suicide rate over the past 20 years. Within the large group of school-age children are subgroups that have a much higher rate of suicide than the rate for the entire group. For example, troubled adolescents have been estimated to attempt suicide at a rate of 33% (Tomlinson-Keasey & Keasey, 1988). From these studies, we can conclude that the rate of adolescent suicide has risen over the past decade, as have the rates of other groups. We can also conclude that subgroups vary in their rate of suicide.

A significant contribution of previous research on adolescent suicide has been the determination that there are significant risk factors:

- psychiatric disorders, such as depression and anxiety;
- drug and alcohol abuse;
- genetic factors;
- family loss or disruption;
- friend or family member of suicide victim;
- homosexuality;
- rapid sociocultural change;
- media emphasis on suicide;
- impulsiveness and aggressiveness; and
- ready access to lethal methods (Davidson & Linnoila, 1991).

One question I am often asked is whether the suicide rates of gifted adolescents differ significantly from the larger population of adolescents. In my own research, colleagues and I have conducted psychological autopsies of three gifted adolescents who committed suicide. In our literature review, we found several interesting patterns.

The first pattern was the tendency for authors to make conclusions and recommendations about the incidence and nature of gifted suicide without supporting data. Moreover, general findings from marginally related studies were used to support the contention that the rate of suicide among gifted adolescents is the same as or lower than the larger population of adolescents. Again, these statements were based on no direct evidence.

The second pattern was the tendency of authors to cite each other's work based upon speculation. The net effect was the reification of that speculation. This pattern exists throughout research bodies and is not unique to this lore. What makes this research body different is that there is virtually no true research at the foundation of the base, yet truisms abound.

A third and more subtle pattern in the lore was the tendency for authors to advocate for gifted children. Some of the pieces seemed less like efforts at research and more like efforts at protecting the image of gifted children.

Gifted Suicide Rates

Let me reiterate what was most often suggested in the literature: that the suicide rate of gifted adolescents is the same as or lower than the general population of adolescents. The basis for this claim is conceptual, not empirical. In fact, there is so little evidence available about gifted adolescents on this specific topic that nothing should be concluded. In other words, at this point, we cannot know.

Although seemingly an innocuous difference in assessments, the ramifications can vary significantly. For example, there is a growing number of academics considering the population of gifted adolescents in smaller, more representative subgroups than in an omnibus fashion. In this case, students with differing characteristics might have markedly different incidents of suicide during adolescence. Some evidence for this claim can be found in research that has studied the lives of a large group of eminent people in the artistic and literary world. Among this subgroup, Ludwig (1995) found a higher incidence of suicide by the age of 30. He also found that "investigative types" (e.g., scientists) committed suicide at a higher rate than the general population after the age of 60.

I must interject a serious note of caution here. These data were drawn from a much older population, and, given the nature of the risk factors often associated with suicide, there may be a limited ability to generalize the findings. So, even though it stands to reason that subgroups of adolescents are at greater risk of committing suicide than other groups, there is not enough evidence to conclude whether or not gifted adolescents *per se* have a higher-than-average risk.

Some Reasons There Are Few Studies to Draw On

There are several reasons why there have been few studies conducted on the suicides of gifted students. A few include:

- the current data collected nationally about adolescent suicide do not include whether or not the individual was gifted;
- the varying definitions of giftedness and talent used across the United States make it difficult to know whether a child who committed suicide was gifted;
- issues of confidentiality limit access to data;
- conducting psychological autopsies of suicide victims is an expensive endeavor in terms of time and money;
- the fact that more adolescents than preadolescents commit suicide combined with the fact that secondary schools are not as actively engaged in identifying gifted students makes conducting research on this topic more difficult; and
- the terminal nature of suicide requires certain types of information to be garnered after the event.

Promising Studies

I am aware of a handful of studies that show promise of contributing to the research lore in significant ways. Two looked specifically at suicide ideation, one at the secondary level and one among honors students in college. A third study showing promise is the psychological autopsies previously noted. Combined, they will add significantly to the current level of understanding.

One interesting question that recognizes human variation within the gifted population deals with a topic of considerable debate among academics. That is, "What specific role, if any, do the qualities that some gifted adolescents possess play in their suicides?" For example, possible connections between gifted children's unusual sensitivities and perfectionism (Delisle, 1986) and isolationism and introversion (Kaiser & Berndt, 1985) with suicidal behavior have been raised. In the psychological autopsies being conducted, we have found that Piechowski's treatment of Dabrowski's theories have been helpful in interpreting the data collected. Some of the characteristics we have found beneficial in the data-analysis phase include intellectual-introspection, avid reading, curiosity, imaginational-fantasy, animistic and magical thinking, mixing truth and fiction, illusions, being emotional, strong affective memory, concern with death, depressive and suicidal moods, sensitivity in relationships, and feelings of inadequacy and inferiority (Piechowski, 1979).

What can we say about the suicides of gifted adolescents?

- Adolescents are committing suicide.
- Gifted adolescents are committing suicide.
- The rate of suicide has increased over the past decade for the general population of adolescents within the context of an over-all increase across all age groups.
- It is reasonable to conclude that the incidence of suicide of gifted adolescents has increased over the past decade while keeping in mind that there are no definitive data on the subject.
- Given the limited data available, we cannot ascertain whether the incidence of suicide among gifted adolescents is different from the incidence among the general population of adolescents.

For Discussion

- How would you respond to the question: Are the suicide rates among gifted adolescents different than nongifted adolescents?

- Reflect on and discuss the limitations associated with studying gifted adolescent suicide.

On Chance
and Being
Gifted

Key Concepts

- Psychobiological influences
- Cultural influences
- Sociohistorical influences
- Family variables in context

Gifted students are the most diverse (heterogeneous) group of people to study because they can vary the most on the most number of variables.

This chapter examines the role of chance in the lives of gifted students. More specifically, it illustrates how being gifted—whether or not one is identified as being gifted and the experience of being gifted—is affected by a particular chance factor. Specific examples are used to illustrate different manifestations of chance factors that affect the lives of gifted students. Because there are so many chance factors that potentially affect the psychological development of gifted students, I have sorted them into categories. For example, there are genetic, lifestyle, environmental, overarching vs. instance, experiential, and coincidental chance factors.

The most obvious examples are the chance variables associated with the genetic makeup of a gifted child's parents. The point of noting this factor is to emphasize the sheer power of the psychobiological influence of the gifted child that is a function of the genetic makeup of the parents. Consequently, when children are born, they are not really a clean slate; they have many predispositions, tendencies, and potentialities.

Another important chance factor is the location of a child's birth and upbringing. Imagine an intellectually gifted child born in Stockholm, Paris, Milledgeville, Moosejaw, Trinidad, the Shoshoni and Arapaho Reservation, and so forth. Clearly, each location has significantly different histories and cultures. Hence, where gifted children happen to be born affects whether and how they might be identified as gifted and what their experiences will be.

When a gifted child is born is also quite significant. For example, imagine being a gifted student in science and math in the late 1950s in the United States. Because of the political uproar after the launch of Sputnik, great interest and money was put into gifted education in math and science. Now, imagine the same gifted child whose abilities were in language arts. Little interest existed at that time for those gifts.

Another example brings the topic closer to home. I call it "the family variables in context." Imagine a gifted girl, Jane, whose extraordinary skills are in the area of language arts. She lives in a medium-sized city in the United States. Her father is deceased, her mother works two full-time jobs at minimum wage to support the family of four, health care is not provided, and, at age 9, she is the oldest child and therefore often misses school to help care for the other children. All three children spend hours without adult supervision, and minimal books are available in the home.

Another gifted child, Tony, lives in a small rural community. He attends second grade in a school of 50 students in grades K–12. There are two teachers and one aide for the entire school. Tony's parents are ranchers on a small plot of land. The family has no television or computer. The boy's extraordinary abilities are in math.

Tony's new friend is a gifted boy named Juan whose parents are employed as migrant farm workers. They only live in Tony's farming community for about 2 months a year. At other times of the year, Juan's family moves across three other states. Juan likes Tony's town, partly because he gets to go to school there.

The last example of a gifted child is Brenda, a 16-year-old who is top in her school class. She is also an outstanding athlete. Both parents are well-educated; her father is a brilliant college professor. She has lived her life in a small college town and has grown up spending a great deal of time on the university campus. The family lives in a fine house with several computers and hundreds of books.

What is remarkable about the examples of Jane, Tony, Juan, and Brenda is that they are real people living in the same state—Wyoming—at the same time in history (names were changed to protect their anonymity). Implicit in using these life cases to illustrate different children with gifts and talents is the importance that chance factors play in the individual child's capacity to reach his or her potential. Given the information shared about these children, it is clear that their own potential and specific qualities *per se* have little to do with the likelihood of their reaching their potential. Rather, it is easy to see how chance factors have played a significant role in their lives to date. However, the fact that they were identified as gifted and were receiving (what I deemed to be) appropriate gifted education services creates hope because it means that the myriad forms of variation in conditions and types of abilities that have been described were still understandable to professional educators who work in the schools of Wyoming. So, while genetic makeup cannot be transcended, it does not have to create insurmountable hurdles to identifying and serving gifted students. We merely need to remind ourselves that our science and pedagogy must emanate from the idea that gifted students are the most diverse group of people to study because they can vary on the most number of variables. The fact that chance exists in so many ways means that the training of school personnel must recognize and attend to these factors.

One of the most powerful chance factors that affects gifted children is the socioeconomic status (SES) of their parents. The research on SES and achievement is clear: There are certain factors of poverty that mitigate against school success. I contend that the achievement gaps between what is possible and what is actually accomplished among our gifted students from the poorest families is the greatest of any group of students. Although everyone can agree that all students should be expected to reach their potential, gifted students from the lowest SES are at the greatest risk for underachievement. And, as the brief case descriptions of a small number of gifted students in Wyoming illustrates, the poor gifted child, although quite diverse in background and circumstances, can be identified and serviced.

Why were teachers in the schools in Wyoming able to meet the needs of the gifted students described above? The state struggles with severe financial swings in its economy, which affect its schools. It is a largely rural state with many one-room schools remaining. Many years ago, when I served as president of the Wyoming Association for Gifted Education (WAGE), it was clear that school districts had differing definitions of giftedness and programs were often created, lived, thrived, and ended on the basis of an individual teacher's work. I participated in numerous discussions with long-term teachers of the gifted who revealed many of the same difficulties most states experience today. For example, they described feeling alone in their commitment to gifted students; that there was not enough money to work on behalf of gifted students and too little general support provided by administrators; that the state department did not emphasize gifted education enough; that they did not have enough resources; and that, because there was only one university in the state to provide training, too little training was available to them. Even with all these potential limitations, the teachers were able to identify the various manifestations of giftedness, understand the other chance factors that affected gifted students' abilities to reach their potential, and then create learning conditions that were appropriate and beneficial.

I believe that some intangible factors that exist in the unique state of Wyoming are important in understanding why the teachers were so successful. The state was settled by independent people who endured certain hardships to live there. I also think that the state's history of accommodating vast differences among its students is due to the degree of rurality of the state and its history of one-room schools. These factors created a mindset that "teaching to the needs of each child" must be the rule, rather than the exception. Therefore, some of the tenets of differentiation existed in Wyoming long before the recent resurgence of the concept.

The field of gifted education has evolved over the years to the point where many advocate a gifted services model, rather than a specific programmatic model. The former has the advantage of being able to attend to the individual needs of students as compared to the latter example, which generally requires identification approaches that match a type of gifted student to a typically narrowly conceived program. An ongoing limitation with the programmatic model is the inherent limitations of schools of not having enough programs to accommodate all gifted students. In small schools, a critical mass of students has proven to limit specific programs that are offered. This evolution lends itself to schools being better suited to deal with the diversity that gifted students manifest, including their chance variables. Assuming attention is paid to the goal of accommodating all needs of gifted students in school, then Jane, Tony, Juan, and Brenda's needs can be met. Allegiance to programs is not the same as allegiance to students. The first step school personnel need to take is to accept the challenge of meeting all needs of all gifted students. Secondly, educators need to understand fully the diversity of giftedness. The third step is to be able to identify as many chance factors as possible, separating those that are to the advantage of the gifted student from the ones that cannot be dealt with. To accomplish this, the child's psychological development will need to be considered in a sophisticated manner. A planned set of services that draw on any necessary resources available to the teacher will become the tools of the trade. In other words, the classroom becomes the home base, not the student's entire world.

Imagine the scope of benefits we can bring to the lives of students with gifts and talents by reducing any negative effects that chance factors play in their lives.

For Discussion

- The influence of the Sputnik launch on gifted education was mentioned. Discuss other sociohistorical events and their influence on gifted education.

- Which of the following chance factors do you consider to be the most influential on the development of a gifted child: psychobiological, cultural, sociohistorical, or parents' socioeconomic status? Explain why.

Guiding
Gifted
Children

Once we know a little about who gifted children are, it is important for us to use that knowledge to help them function successfully in their environment.

The chapters in this section focus on what I believe is important in this guidance process. The first three chapters—"Guiding and Supporting the Development of Gifted Children," "Practical Advice for Guiding the Gifted," and "Working on Behalf of Gifted Students"— offer ideas about things teachers, parents, and counselors should consider in their role and some specific things they can do for their young charges. I allude to the important role of communication in many of the suggestions listed in these first three chapters, and, in the fourth, "Developing Relationships, Communication, and Identity," I focus on how it can be a difficult aspect of childhood. Communicating with the adults in their lives, building relationships with other children, and developing their own sense of identity are all aspects of childhood that can be traumatic or relatively easy. This chapter gives some suggestions for smoothing the path for gifted children.

In the fifth chapter of this section, "Putting the Well-Being of All Students (Including Gifted Students) First," I explore the concept of well-being and what this means for gifted students in the school context. The final chapter in this section also focuses on the school environment. In "Gifted Students and the Adults Who Provide for Them: Lessons Learned from Terrorism," I examine the reactions and coping strategies of the academically gifted adolescents at the Indiana Academy for Science, Mathematics, and Humanities following the September 11, 2001 terrorist attacks. I then discuss the lessons learned from this tragedy in relation to guiding the social and emotional development of gifted students.

Guiding and Supporting the Development of Gifted Children

Key Concepts

- Strategies exist for guiding and supporting gifted students.
- Adults' best efforts cannot prevent all the struggles and emotional turmoil from occurring in a child's life.
- A gifted child is a child first.
- Communication among groups of adults is vital.
- Try to understand the social milieu of the school.
- Serve as a clearinghouse for information about gifted students.
- Learn about the gifted child's personality and social goals.
- Teach the child to better understand him- or herself.
- Provide opportunities for gifted children to be together.

Having spent several years conducting research, working directly with gifted students in the role of teacher, counselor, and program director, and reading others' studies on the topic of the social and emotional needs of gifted students, I have come to believe that there are several strategies that will help parents, teachers, and counselors guide gifted children.

Some of the topics have a substantial research base, some have only a modest research base, and some have little to no published research base supporting them. Cutting across these ideas is a form of conventional wisdom that I have seen expressed by many in the field. I suspect the reason that such widespread conventional wisdom exists is primarily due to the fact that our professional experiences become our primary source of data as we try to make sense of the world. Although I believe there is danger in relying too much on personal experiences when making generalizations, I do respect the fact that drawing on multiple forms of data, including personal experience, is an appropriate method for making informed decisions. So, to break with my past practice of trying to forward only those ideas that have emerged from published research findings, I am going to provide a partial list of ideas that I believe have merit when trying to guide gifted children.

I will let my qualifiers reflect the degree of confidence that I have in these ideas. Some are speculative, while others are soundly supported by a research base. Some are taken from research in gifted education, some from outside the field, and some come largely from my own professional experience. Consider these ideas for teachers, counselors, and parents who guide the social and emotional development of gifted children:

1. As you consider your role in the development of a gifted child, realize that your best efforts cannot prevent all the struggles and emotional turmoil from occurring in the child's life. Your efforts may, however, allow the child to effectively transcend the difficulties associated with youth, and particularly those issues unique to gifted children.

2. Remember that the gifted child is a child first. Adults often forget that the young person with whom they are dealing is, in fact, a child. When listening to gifted children talk about academic topics, it is difficult to remember that they are very likely at the same general developmental level in the social and emotional domain as their nongifted peers. Treat children as young people first, and deal with their specific gifts second.

3. Communication among the three groups of adults (parents, teachers, counselors) is vital. Each group needs a clear understanding of the child and the parents' and teacher's goals for the child. These three groups of adults often have different goals for the students. Consequently, it is important to share appropriate information.

4. Try to understand the social milieu of the school or classroom through the eyes of the child. This is a difficult, but worthwhile task. I have been astounded and dismayed by the extent to which the social expectations for students are never openly discussed or understood. Often, the teacher and other school personnel have quite divergent views of what it means to be a student or a gifted student. Moreover, students also hold a wide variety of opinions about what they think being a student means and how they should behave in various school settings. Therefore, talking openly about the expectations for students can help them feel more comfortable in the school.

5. Serve as a clearinghouse for information about gifted students. Share the information via meetings and by sharing literature. Since none of the three groups of adults (parents, teachers, counselors) receives significant training on the nature and needs of gifted students, it is important to create opportunities for them to learn how to be proactive in the child's life. The ERIC Clearinghouse has invaluable information prepared for this purpose. Other sources of information include local colleges and universities, state agencies, the National Association for Gifted Children, the Association for the Gifted, and the Internet.

6. Make available individual, group, and family counseling for gifted students and their families. Although relatively easy to organize, it is rarely done. If this is difficult to arrange, then share materials with each group (parents, teachers, counselors) as a means to better prepare the various professionals who work with gifted children.

7. Learn about the child's personality and social goals. This will enable all three groups to guide the child through the school years. When pursuing this strategy, be sure to include information from the field of "general" psychology. The vast majority of facts within the field of psychology are applicable to the lives of gifted students.

8. Teach the child to better understand his or her nature and anticipate how to react to events and circumstances in his or her life. Part of this understanding may be accomplished through personality and interest inventories. Astute adults in positions to provide observationally based information may also be helpful to the child. This strategy calls for three groups of adults to work together.

9. Provide opportunities for gifted children to be together. This opportunity seems to alleviate some of the pressures a gifted child feels. For example, gifted students often report feeling different from other students, except when they have time to be together with other gifted students. When together, they often comment on the profound sense of relief of knowing there are other people like themselves who have many similar interests and qualities.

I hope you find some of these ideas helpful as you work on behalf of gifted children. The next chapters will continue this list of ideas to consider about the social and emotional needs of gifted students.

For Discussion

- Consider the social expectations for a gifted preadolescent. In what way are they different from (or similar to) the social expectations of the gifted adolescent?

- Discuss the social milieu of the school or classroom with a gifted girl and a gifted boy. Are the social expectations different for girls and boys? How did the social milieu of the school from their perspectives differ from your perspective?

Practical Advice
for Guiding
the Gifted

Key Concepts

- Recognize and respect the relationship between social and emotional needs and academic needs.
- Be cautious about forcing your desires on students based on your perception of their strength areas.
- Teach pro-social skill development.
- Teach them to enjoy nonacademic activities.
- Teach gifted students ways to manage stress.
- Adults should model the behavior they wish gifted students to exhibit.
- Do not try to change the basic nature of the student.
- Embrace diversity, do not merely tolerate it.
- Expose gifted students to knowledgeable counseling.
- Know that coping strategies exist.
- Provide opportunities for down time.

The following was originally written to be the second installment in a three-part series on the social and emotional needs of gifted students. In the series, I broke with my past practice of trying to only forward ideas that have emerged from published research findings.

Below are some ideas to consider as teachers, counselors, and parents attempt to guide the social and emotional development of gifted children.

1. Recognize and respect the relationship between social and emotional needs and academic needs. One affects the other. For example, whether a gifted student is challenged or able to work at a pace that is stimulating can affect his or her emotional well-being. Our school psychology clinic in Teachers College at Ball State University has documented that the most common reason gifted students are referred for psychological assessments is rooted in their becoming a behavior problem in school after having previously been a strong student. The root of the behavioral change is the manifest frustration with not being challenged in school. For many students, this connection goes unnoticed until it is far too late to help them.

2. Be cautious about forcing your desires on students based on your perception of their strength areas. Talent manifests over time and with opportunity. Determining for a child what his or her "gift" or "talent" is without allowing for flexibility or encouraging additional self-exploration may cause a number of problems from adolescence on. A positive outcome of nurturing a talent is the development of a lifelong avocational interest or hobby.

3. Teach prosocial skill development. Teaching gifted students a handful of social skills can reduce the number of negative experiences they may encounter while in school. The phrasing of questions and comments and the ability to take another person's perspective are skills that are helpful in teaching gifted students to navigate the difficult social waters in schools.

4. Teach them to enjoy nonacademic activities. As appropriate, try to teach gifted students to recognize that nonacademic pursuits are also important in one's life. They become stress relievers and additional areas where gifted students can grow. Modeling works well in teaching this lesson.

5. Teach gifted students ways to manage stress. As they move through the grades, many will experience growing amounts of stress.

Ironically, much of this will be self-imposed or a consequence of only their gift being recognized by those around them without concern for their needs as individuals. Because many gifted students develop coping strategies, educating them about how to effectively manage stress may prove relatively easy.

6. To accomplish many of the suggestions previously noted, adults should model the behavior they wish gifted students to exhibit. Like all children, gifted students learn from the behavior of adults. Whether it is effective coping strategies, nonthreatening communication techniques, or how to relax, teachers, counselors, and parents often become the models that children follow. If you want your messages to be influential, let the students see you behaving accordingly.

7. Understand that much of how gifted students appear and behave is biologically affected. Do not try to change the basic nature of the student. Shyness, for example, like some physical characteristics, has roots in biology. Like the relationship between body type and weight, shyness and a student's willingness and ability to actively participate in class are related. Respect the nature of the individual gifted child.

8. Embrace diversity, do not merely tolerate it. To tolerate suggests a position of authority or position of judgment that allows someone to decide what human differences are meaningful and, therefore, acceptable and what differences are intolerable. This special privileged position tends to disadvantage gifted students because giftedness rarely makes people's lists of meaningful differences. As a teacher, parent, or counselor, you are in a position to have a significant impact on the minds of gifted children. If a school truly embraces diversity, then gifted students will be accepted. In many schools, giftedness is still experienced as being aberrant. In a study a few years ago, I found that gifted students are just as prone to believe stereotypical ideas about other gifted students as the general population. This phenomenon can be explained by the fact that gifted students cannot escape their environment.

9. Expose gifted students to knowledgeable counseling—avoid professionals who are not knowledgeable about gifted students. A proac-

tive counseling program can be invaluable to gifted students. Learning about oneself and how to effectively relate to others in school can positively affect the psychological development of gifted students. Conversely, messages learned from untrained counselors and psychologists who rely on intuition when providing services can actually exacerbate problems in the social and emotional realm.

10. Know that many gifted students will have created coping strategies while in the earliest grades in school. I have found that, by first grade, some gifted children have begun to engage in behavior patterns that reveal their discomfort with the gifted student label. Some of these strategies reflect their tacit knowledge about the social milieu of their classroom. Knowing that these patterns exist can enable teachers, counselors, and parents to understand the worries and behaviors surrounding gifted students' school experience.

11. Provide opportunities for down time. All children need time to relax away from school concerns. Arranging down time for some students will come easy, but for others it will be quite difficult. Providing gifted students opportunities to explore or read for pleasure can reduce stress and may have the positive effect of increasing avocational pursuits when they get older.

I hope you find some of these suggestions beneficial as you attempt to meet the social and emotional needs of gifted students. The next chapter will provide yet another list of considerations for parents, teachers, and counselors as they attempt the important task of meeting the psychological, social, and emotional needs of gifted students.

For Discussion

- Reflect on some behaviors that you (as a parent, teacher, or counselor) model that are beneficial (or not so beneficial) for a gifted child or student.

- Ask the school psychologist or counselor what training she or he has in gifted education.

Working on Behalf of Gifted Students

<table>
<tr><td align="center">**Key Concepts**</td></tr>
</table>

Key Concepts
• Social risk taking • Diversity in education • Importance of reading biographies • Mentoring • Importance of nonacademic interests • Identity foreclosure

The following appeared as the third column in a series on meeting the social and emotional needs of gifted students. A number are somewhat specific to gifted students, while others might be as effective with students of average ability. Some of the ideas respect biological influences while others emphasize environmental influences in this area. Clearly, only some of the ideas expressed across the three-part series will be relevant for any specific student given his or her particular circumstances in life. Consequently, adults need to assess the salience of the ideas before attempting to pursue them.

1. Encourage controlled risk taking. Although it may seem on the surface to be an oxymoron, it really is not. Imagine the lives of profes-

sional stunt men and women. People who earn a living by risking their lives do so with careful planning. They take obvious risks to their physical well-being, but they do so after great effort has gone into building safety nets that minimize the potential for their harm. Similarly, gifted students need to take risks to build same- and opposite-sex friendships and communicate with other students and teachers. To engage in this type of social risk taking, safeguards need to be in place. Parents, teachers, and counselors can create those safety nets with preparation. For example, building an accepting environment in a classroom and school establishes a climate that supports emotional and social risk taking. This suggestion dovetails into the next one.

2. Provide myriad social experiences for gifted students. In concert, the three groups of adults can orchestrate varied situations where gifted students interact with a wide variety of people. These types of experiences will build social skills specific to contexts and have the effect of developing the gifted students' social cognition. As the students have positive experiences, their self-concepts will also be enhanced.

3. Inventory family similarities and differences as compared to schoolmates. In some school settings, the diversity is obvious, while in others it is not. It can be helpful to gifted students for their parents, particularly, but also for teachers and counselors, to let them know what their family's values, practices, and beliefs are and how they vary across groups of people. If done within the context of diversity, then their giftedness can be accepted as quite normal, rather than aberrant.

4. To accomplish the previous suggestion, one approach is to encourage the reading of biographies of eminent people. This is considered a form of bibliotherapy. The details provided in the biographies will often cause two events to occur. The consciousness of the gifted student will be raised concerning the experiences the eminent person had that impacted his or her development. For example, some of the scientists in Germany prior to World War II speak about their lives as Jews during the rise of Hitler and the strong anti-Semitism that pervaded Germany. The second event that often occurs is the combination of comparing the reader's life with that of the person in the biography, and then the awareness that many highly accomplished people also struggled with some of the same issues affecting the

reader's life. This realization tends to reduce feelings of isolation while at the same time providing ideas for dealing with the difficulties gifted people encounter. Part of the potential effectiveness of the bibliotherapy approach is that the reader becomes actively engaged and creates his or her own understanding. This is a vastly different experience from having one's parent discuss issues with you. Although both reading biographies and discussing with parents can be successful, using both approaches may prove more beneficial than relying on only one.

5. A second approach for educating about diversity is to provide mentorship opportunities for gifted students. Apprenticeships can have many positive effects, including numerous ones in the skill-building domain. In this example, it is important to note the connection with the life story aspect of psychological development. For example, working with a mentor teaches many lessons, including who is the mentor and what pathway he or she followed to become what he or she is from the mentor's own perspective. Through this person's life story, salient issues in the individual development of the mentor can be recognized and understood by the gifted student. Like the effects of bibliotherapy, connecting with a significant adult who represents an academic area of interest to a gifted student offers many opportunities for the student to appreciate and navigate the social and emotional waters of his or her life.

6. Love and respect gifted students for who they are. Then, emphasize doing rather than being; ability and talent are neutral constructs, while doing is virtuous. Try to help them understand that being academically able does not make a person good or bad, per se. Rather, like many characteristics one has, it is how one strives to develop and subsequently use other abilities that makes him or her virtuous. It is important for both gifted students and others to develop their talents. Avocational talent is important, too. The overemphasis by the three groups of adults on the students' abilities tends to create feelings by gifted students that they are nothing *but* their academic ability or achievement. This can lead to myriad problems, including underachievement, unnecessary suffering when doing poorly in school, the unwillingness to stretch beyond areas of prior attainment, and identity foreclosure. Identity foreclosure is the result of deciding at too young an age where to emphasize one's professional

aspirations. Deciding to pursue math as a career because early in one's life a person is taught that he or she is particularly able in that area will often lead to the student choosing not to risk failure in other areas. Hence, other potential talent areas are never identified. Negative patterns within careers also exist for many who decided about their career too early in life.

7. Encourage a self-concept that extends far beyond the academic self-concept. It is never beneficial to a gifted student to convince him or her that only academic achievement is valuable. What good to society is a person who can calculate advanced math problems at an early age, but who has developed no civic responsibilities? Although I do not accept the claim that schools should attempt to develop equally the "whole" person, I do believe that gifted students should be appreciated as children who develop over time and, consequently, deserve the right to develop various aspects of their being. As in every preceding example, the three groups of adults need to work together for this suggestion to be realized.

Teachers, parents, and counselors should recognize the important roles they play in the psychological development of gifted students. Gifted students will develop with or without adult guidance. The question is "How will they develop without coordinated guidance that is underpinned by research in developmental psychology and informed research on gifted students' lives in school?" My answer is that it is inconceivable that they can develop as well and as painlessly without the support of the three groups of adults. Let us commit to supporting the psychological development of all students, including gifted students.

For Discussion

- As a teacher, counselor, or parent, consider whether you provide opportunities for social risk taking for gifted individuals.

- Compile a list of three (or more) biographies of gifted individuals that you have read or would like to read. Share them with your classmates to compile an extensive list to use with your student or child.

Developing Relationships, Communication, and Identity

Key Concepts

- Improving communication through journaling and artistic expression
- Building relationships
- Developing identity

For this chapter, I have divided the suggestions that teachers, parents, and counselors can consider as they work on behalf of gifted students into four groups: (1) improving communication, (2) building relationships, (3) developing identity, and (4) for the adults. Many of the ideas are equally applicable to gifted students and students of average ability.

Improving Communication

One of the most effective approaches to improving the communication between gifted students and adults, and between gifted students and other students, is to encourage the expression of thoughts and feelings.

For many years, journaling has been used to elicit ideas and the exchange of thoughts and feelings between a teacher and student. It has also been used by therapists to gain insight into the client and to assist the client in the self-reflection process. The communication among both groups (students/adults, students/other students) can be improved through journaling when the adult establishes goals for the student's journals and encourages the participation of the student.

A simple note of warning is called for here. Attempting to improve communication by reading a student's private journal (diary) will hurt rather than improve communication. The student is likely to feel violated by the adult, and he or she will most likely minimize communication for some period of time afterward.

Another way to improve communication is to create opportunities for the student to express him- or herself through artistic means. Again, this approach has a long, rich history in the field of psychology as a means of reaching difficult clients and in helping clients heal. I strongly encourage adults to use these techniques as stimuli only and not as diagnostic tools. The immediate benefit will be derived from the conversations enabled by the process and products, not due to any diagnosis made by the adult.

Building Relationships

The second set of suggestions is offered as a means to help gifted students build relationships with other people, both students and adults. Gifted students often feel that they have few friends with similar interests. Technological breakthroughs, particularly the use of electronic mail, has made communicating with others around the globe both immediate and inexpensive. I encourage the adults to look for ways to assist in the interactions of gifted students with others via e-mail.

This process is becoming increasingly common as teachers have their students create electronic pen pals as part of class assignments. These relationships are typically well-managed and quite safe for the students. Friendly relationships emerge as a natural consequence of gifted students meeting others like themselves. Tales abound of the friendships created during specialized programs such as Governor's Schools or other summer residential programs that are sustained by using e-mail.

The more traditional approach of encouraging pen pal relationships still provides options for gifted students to build relationships with others who have similar interests. The traditional approach adds an additional level of safety, although it sacrifices the immediacy of using electronic mail. Both can work, but both need adult supervision.

In addition to developing relationships with other people, many benefits can be derived from involving the student with a pet. The relationship that often develops between children and pets is known to be very important in students' development of personal responsibility, compassion, and empathy. There can also be benefits from basic companionship.

Developing Identity

There are numerous ways of assisting in the development of a student's identity. Some are relatively easy to bring about, while others are much more difficult. Many adults may be unaware that gifted children often become concerned with ethical considerations of life at an earlier age than is common for most children. Adults are often surprised by the child's concerns, and sometimes they will make light of them. Anticipating and dealing honestly and empathetically with young children who are struggling with these worries can be very important to their development.

Gifted students should be encouraged to have an active life outside of school. There are benefits to outside activities that remain separate from school and those that have some connection to school. For example, learning to play musical instruments can originate in or out of school, and the potential transfer back and forth is generally a positive experience in building identity. Other parallel experiences include sports-related activities, such as soccer, baseball, football, and so forth. Sports, for those interested, can help develop a positive sense of identity. I do, however, stress the need for the child to be interested. Few experiences are more difficult for children than to fail repeatedly in front of friends, family, and other people. Lack of interest, even when a student has ability, does not nurture skills development. This leaves them vulnerable to embarrassment.

A third suggestion is to respect the passions of the children, especially as they grow older. With young children, parents effectively control the children's activities. Consequently, the children tend to have options that are of some interest to their families.

As the students get older, they are allowed to explore more, potentially developing interests outside of their parents' desires. Balancing the time and energy needed to develop any area of endeavor is difficult. Parents need to allow the time for interests to develop, even when they are not the parents' interests. Respecting the passions of gifted students will assist in the development of their self-concepts and feelings of self-efficacy and agency.

A very important quality for healthy adults is empathy. Some gifted children have an abundance of empathy, while others need to be taught. Teaching empathy is not easy, but it can be done.

As noted in a previous chapter, helping develop a sophisticated understanding of human diversity can reduce the pain and suffering of gifted children as they realize that being different is both the norm and the exception; the norm in the infinite ways people differ, and the exception when one is seeking people who have similar interests, qualities, or beliefs.

Empathy for the lives of others enables gifted children to more fully appreciate that people have psychological needs that are similar to their own. Without empathy, gifted children can come to believe that they are completely estranged from others since the more obvious differences (e.g., academic passions) will dominate their perspectives of others.

One approach to developing empathy is to engage the child in an activity where each person assumes the perspective of another. Over time, the conditions can be changed so that difficult situations can be experienced vicariously to the extent necessary to build empathy.

For the Adults

The final category I have titled "for the adults." I include these suggestions because an unintended implication is that, if you follow the ideas outlined in this chapter, the gifted child will not suffer. As a psychologist, researcher, and parent, the hardest lesson I have had to learn is the inevitability of pain and suffering experienced by gifted children. This realization can elicit feelings of inadequacy and impotence in the adults around them.

I encourage the three groups of adults to work diligently to assist in the development of gifted children, but to be prepared for the difficulties of life. Constant communication can have a positive impact since many of life's difficulties will emerge from the child interacting in the adults' environments. Modeling calmness and caring may prove to be the best practice in which one can engage when the students are suffering with the normal trials and tribulations of life.

By being aware of the social and emotional needs of our young people, we will be better able to effectively guide their development. Let us continue to attempt to help all children enjoy rich and full lives, including gifted children.

For Discussion

- Reflect on whether you provide opportunities for gifted children/students to express themselves artistically. Do you encourage them to participate in activities that are unrelated to their "talent" or "gift"?

Putting the Well-Being of All Students (Including Gifted Students) First

---

Key Concepts

- The meaning of *well-being*
- Well-being for gifted children in the school context
- Learning at appropriate rates and in appropriate environments

---

What if we put the well-being of the individual student (including gifted students) first in planning and carrying out school activities? How would things be different? These two questions seem innocuous at first, but upon further inspection, the answers may, in fact, require radical departures from current thinking and practice.

Preface

In my judgment, one of the most existential events that occurs in one's life is learning. *Existentialism* is defined as a "philosophical theory emphasizing the existence of the individual person as a free and responsible agent determining his or her own development" (Allen, 1996, p. 506). We do it by ourselves. An individual must change in order to learn. We can either facilitate or impede learning, but only the individual can literally make it happen. In essence, learning is a personal experience that professional educators should try to facilitate by bringing to bear the best educational practices known. Sometimes this requires us to reconsider our beliefs and practices. One such question is "What if we put the well-being of the individual student (including gifted students) first in planning and carrying out school activities?"

Let us begin by noting the arguments that many have leveled against the idea of schools putting the well-being of individuals first: (1) We cannot organize schools around the needs of every student individually; (2) this would be too expensive, too difficult, too cumbersome, and too complicated; (3) it would cause too many scheduling problems; (4) it would hurt sports or band; and (5) why have it as a goal anyway because (gifted) students need to learn how to adapt to the real world, rather than expecting the world to adapt to their needs? I lump these concerns under the heading of "ideas that require school leaders to move beyond their comfort zone" and, therefore, generally fail.

Context

So, what if schools focused on the well-being of their gifted students as individuals first? Before they could do that, a few questions would need to be answered. For example, what does well-being mean? Most schools already claim to look after the well-being of all their students; they just do not ascribe to the goal of individual needs driving decision making and determining practice. In essence, we abrogate decisions on defining well-being to local school boards and state departments of education. This then gets handed off to the growing number of states' minimum-competency tests. Hence, *well-being* is often defined as reaching minimum competency on a statewide achievement test, a definition that rarely has positive effects in the lives of gifted students. Local school districts decide how to spend their budget to assist their students in reaching minimum competency. As the old saying goes, "we measure what we treasure." Question: How many states' minimum-competency testing initiatives were originated by teachers? None. Typically, state legislatures create bills to this end. These efforts are usually supported, if not pushed, by state chambers of commerce. Hence, a competing notion of well-being from state's financial communities is often that our students are part of the equation that should provide business owners a competitive edge. Consequently, children are educated at the same time that two very different notions of what is in their best interest are being held. It would be nice to think that battles are raging over these competing ideas, but unfortunately the commerce-based notion of well-being has ended the argument with the advent of minimum-competency testing.

It was recently reported in an Indiana newspaper that state legislators are seeking a law that would criminalize any behavior under the heading of improper testing practices—including teaching to the test—relative to the state's achievement test. If this occurs, teachers whose livelihood is already contingent upon the scores of their students on this minimum-competency test, could go to jail if they teach to the test. How does this position stack up with another significant national educational movement, often sponsored by those who wish to determine school outcomes—The College Board? More specifically, Advanced Placement (AP) courses, their respective tests, and the faculty members who teach the courses, could not be more closely interconnected. AP faculty regularly use practice tests made up of items from previous exams, and are encouraged to do so. In addition, they are asked to grade vast numbers of the same tests their own students take. So, why is teaching to the test at the minimum competency level so scandalous, and at the most advanced level of instruction, desirable? Teachers are "damned if you do; and damned if you don't." I guess the key is timing. Ironically, neither of these approaches put the individual student's needs first.

De Facto Goals of Schools

As is always the case, we have intrepid teachers who want what is best for their students. They move within the culture of their schools, districts, state rules and regulations, and under the umbrella of their states' minimum-competency testing expectations. Although there is clear evidence that many teachers are willing to experiment with their organization and pedagogy on behalf of students, it has historically been a problem that some of the recommended practices on behalf of gifted students exceed the individual teacher's ability to act. For example, grade skipping (single and multiple) and course skipping depend upon support from other teachers and administrators. They also depend upon the wishes of parents—an important consideration when weighing these two options. Teachers have responded to these and other concerns by literally and metaphorically shutting their classroom doors. This is a reaction to external limitations and a desire to control their own classroom environment, an environment that is subject to the preferences of a number of political and education based groups. While sometimes a necessity, it often reflects few options or support for gifted students to have an individualized education.

Making matters even more difficult for teachers are the expectations we have of them. James Gallagher once told me that teachers of gifted children are expected to be experts in all manifestations of how children vary and are expected to be able to teach them just as effectively across all setting variables. In other words, our students must rely on the standard that every single teacher of the gifted must be extraordinary for the system to work.

Classroom Options

What is left for gifted students in this closed-door environment? Individual teacher attention, a differentiated curriculum, and cluster grouping are a few options available to the teacher. Outside options, such as Saturday and summer special programs, after-school clubs and activities, and mentorships, may also remain. In short, teachers have only some control over whether a school will try to meet the needs of individual students, gifted included.

Social and Emotional Lessons Learned

This model has inherent limitations on gifted students. For example, as the school day progresses, boredom ensues and lessons are learned, such as that being passionate about learning is not valued in school—in fact, it may be counterproductive. Knowledge of the most rudimentary facts and processes are believed to be more valued and welcome in the classroom than advanced knowledge or skills.

How long does it take gifted students to realize that they are going to be taught long before any effort will be made to find out what they already know and are able to do? We turn a collective blind eye to the messages that we send gifted students.

In essence, being passionate about academics holds no currency in schools that plan for the masses and put their focus on minimum-competency tests. What does have a value in their setting? Compliance, complacency, a friendly outgoing personality, and enthusiasm for working in groups are valued. Showing interest and participating in in-the-moment, teacher-led activities, plus "going along," are often the messages learned.

Add to these in-school perceptions the mixed messages that gifted students often perceive, such as "all kids are gifted," "no kids are gifted," "gifted kids have unfair advantages," and "gifted kids can get it on their own," and you have an idea of a gifted child's perceptions. *Child* is the operative word here. Children learn these lessons even when they are unintended. In schools that do not plan for the nature, needs, and knowledge of the individual child, underachievement is prevalent, as is a growing sense of self-doubt and feeling not valued.

Examining Common Terms

Acceleration

With all this as context, what does the commonly used term *acceleration* mean? From the individual child's perspective it does not mean anything. What if we changed the term acceleration to *opportunity to learn at appropriate rates*? It is easy to see the change that perspective makes here. In other words, from the child's perspective, he or she would really experience school as appropriately challenging, but would remain confident when working on the material at hand. This experience is quite the opposite of what is described above and would yield considerable social and emotional benefits to all students, especially gifted students.

Should parents and teachers avoid grade skipping or course skipping out of worries that socially or emotionally a student is not ready; because it would be damaging to the child? Although adults should be concerned about the well-being of their children, this worry is most often a projection of the adults, not a high likelihood. In other words, on what basis is this worry substantiated? At any age and in every classroom, there is a wide variation of children's social development and emotional development. We have all known young children who are socially or emotionally mature or older children who are immature in these areas. Teachers see these variations in their classes daily. Research indicates that only in rare instances are gifted children negatively affected socially or emotionally when they are accelerated. With proper training, teachers should be able to deal effectively with social and emotional variations among their students. Consequently, a student who is able to master the course content more quickly than others should not present a problem when grouped with older students, some of whom may be on the same social or emotional level.

School Mission and Teaching and Administrative Practice

Clearly, people are social beings and schools are learning environments; therefore, schools are social learning environments. Public schools are also institutions supported by tax dollars. Are they intended to be optimal learning environments, the best learning environments that can be had on shoestring budgets, or institutions to prepare less-fortunate children for working-class jobs? Are they led by academic ideals or for social acculturation goals? There are literature bases on all of these examples. Teaching and administrative practice often reveal those intentions that are actually being pursued.

Cooperative Learning

If students have the opportunity to learn at appropriate rates, then what does this say about the practice of cooperative learning? Should students be accelerated to work with students at their same ability level, or should they be grouped with students of lesser ability to work on projects?

Our practices and strategies are based on certain assumptions. Some are tacit while others are known. For example, are cooperative-learning techniques employed as a means to assist in the optimal academic development of each student? I would argue they are not. They represent grouping techniques used for broad social reasons (e.g., gifted students need to learn how to work with less able others, or they will master the subject better by teaching it), a belief that many teachers hold. Cooperative learning is also used with goals of enriching the curriculum. From the student's perspective, however, cooperative learning often teaches gifted students the following lessons:

1. I am expected to do the work of the teacher;
2. The lesson is going to be at a low level; and
3. Extra knowledge and skills are not appreciated in this classroom.

Gifted students often experience being the workhorse for the less serious and capable students in the cooperative-learning groups—they have to carry the group. Does this really happen in schools? As a parent of gifted children, I can report that I have witnessed this as the pattern, rather than the exception, and I have had to counsel my children when they felt great duress after carrying the group.

Acceleration and cooperative learning would mean different things to students if the practice and beliefs surrounding them emerged from the needs of the individual child rather than from so many other influences. Challenging gifted students in highly systematic and informed ways, wherein learning takes place just within the intellectual reach of the child, should be our school's approach. Pretesting before instruction and making decisions about practice and school organization based on the well-being of individual students will improve the learning for all students. This would help to bring out the best in every child (including gifted children), and it would reduce underachievement issues, such as lowered self-concept and feelings of not being valued.

For Discussion

- As a teacher, counselor, or parent, reflect on and discuss how well-being is defined in the school environment. Who defines it?

- Discuss what is done in the school to foster the well-being of gifted children.

Gifted Students and the Adults Who Provide for Them: Lessons Learned From Terrorism

---

Key Concepts

- The need to provide safe, non-prejudicial environments for gifted students
- The importance of good acts and compassion in times of tragedy
- Gifted students must be treated as *people* first
- The importance of regaining control when dealing with major tragedies

---

Every fall, approximately 300 gifted adolescents descend on the Ball State University campus to attend the Indiana Academy for Science, Mathematics, and Humanities (the Academy). The Academy is a state-funded residential school for academically gifted junior and senior high school-aged students. It draws its students from across the state, creating a very diverse community of high-ability learners.

The students come from more than 120 high schools and the transition for the 160 juniors new to the Academy is always difficult. The staff of the school prepare for the onset of counseling and adjustment problems, bringing to bear a great deal of expertise and commitment.

For years, the pattern has been that earliest concerns the Academy counseling staff must attend to revolve around homesickness, minor adjustment problems, roommate concerns, and then, midterms. A week before midterm examinations, the school's student life counselors, coordinator of academic guidance, and supervisor of psychoeducational services experience a rush of students expressing worries about their impending exams. The students are attended to in numerous ways to help them work through the issues concerning them. This pattern was being observed again this year until September 11, 2001. Immediately thereafter, the pattern changed. Like most Americans (and the people of many other countries), Academy students were traumatized. A big difference in 2001 was in the school's ability to provide effective counseling services given the fact that the adults at the Academy were very upset as well. Shock, worry, doubt, and fear were all visible in both the student and the adult faces. The need to provide a safe environment for the students may have been what enabled the school to carry on and the adults to begin the healing process themselves.

Much of the next week was spent providing basic comforts. Innumerable conversations among the students, students and adults, and the adults ensued. Crying was commonplace. Efforts were made to answer questions about the meaning and intention of the event. Many of our regularly scheduled classes were used to discuss the events, and a special volunteer session in the evening was also held. The students were most interested in learning more about the Middle East. Some watched news reports, but many more set out to learn more in other ways, so they could understand better the meaning and significance of the terrible events. The students needed to understand. They needed to know. Very few defaulted to a simplistic understanding based on ignorance or fear. The gifted students needed to know what factors were important to understanding the events of September 11th.

At this same time, a Fulbright Scholar from Saudi Arabia was living at the Academy. His primary goal for being at the Academy was to create a similar school in Saudi Arabia. This person's family was about to follow him to the United States when the terrorist acts occurred. Academy students and staff had grown fond of the visiting scholar, and he was becoming an accepted part of the community. He watched Western and world news reports, showing increasing amounts of upset and depression as the events of September 11th were analyzed. His heart sank as it was reported that many of the parties involved were

Saudis. For six weeks after September 11th, his wife and young daughter were unable to come to the United States to join him. They were very fearful about traveling alone, and about how they might be treated in the West.

The first Friday after the terrorist attacks, our visitor went to pray at the local mosque. Soon after arriving, numerous local preachers and ministers and one police officer arrived. They positioned themselves around the border of the building in an effort to guarantee that those in the mosque could worship freely and with no fear of attack. While there was no indication in the local community that there would have been any problem, the effort was greatly appreciated by those from the mosque, locals, and many who were living and working at the Indiana Academy. Seeing our friend suffer along with us, while at the same time being unable to be with his family gave the acts of terrorism a world perspective that was obvious. The considerate acts from the community members who are often maligned as being uneducated, provincial, too conservative, and even backward, illustrated the importance of good acts in a time of tragedy. It also revealed the mischaracterization of people all over the world by the media. In essence, it reminded us to look at the behavior of people when judging character. The Academy community was keenly aware of the kind, gentle Saudi who was as negatively affected by these events as the rest of us. He came to work every day and modeled acceptance and genuine care for others. His presence at the school provided a daily reminder of the importance of being both compassionate and knowledgeable.

The month following September 11th was very difficult for those living and working at this special residential school. When one considers that all our students move away from their families to live together, along with the fact that the terrorist events are still very disturbing to the adults months later, and will likely become an important emotional milestone for the remainder of our lives, it was a time for lessons to be learned. Learned without the impediments of prejudices or preformed dispositions for how to understand the social and emotional needs of gifted students in our care. As I participated in this community, I tried to be as aware of the interactions among the various groups as possible. I also worked to help orchestrate additional assistance for any person who needed it. Perhaps more importantly, I was constantly facing evidence that supported or contradicted certain aspects of the literature base on the social and emotional needs of gifted students.

Lessons Learned From Terrorism

As has been said many times in the past by caregivers, gifted students must be treated as children first. In our case, however, I will expand that notion by saying that gifted students must be treated as *people* first, the primary distinction here being that providing care for a person is less fraught with age-specific prejudices. Academically gifted junior and senior high-school-aged students can have very powerful intellects. They can also be as emotionally mature or immature as any of their nongifted peers. Hence, to provide for them as a caregiver in the social and emotional domain, these issues must be considered. In other words, dealing only with the human needs, or the human needs in concert with perceived personality or emotional issues taken into consideration are inadequate as strategies. This is especially true when one considers the next issue.

The behavior of the students in the aftermath of the terrorist attacks has reaffirmed for me that many gifted students have a need to understand complicated matters. Aspects of this include the need to understand matters in a thorough and multifaceted way. Other aspects of this need are issues associated with engagement and control. For some, being engaged in the pursuit of understanding is an important part of who they are as a person, and denying them that way of understanding the world is ineffectual counseling practice and potentially harmful in its own right.

Regaining a sense of control when dealing with major tragedies is important to many gifted adolescents. While many professionals who provide counseling services for victims of trauma would say this is true for all people, it can be a little different for intellectually gifted students. For example, regaining a sense of control for many gifted students is affected by the extent to which they are allowed or encouraged to pursue complicated understanding of matters in an intellectual way. Those providing services in times of tragedy should give gifted students opportunities to approach the healing process in this manner. To not do so can exacerbate feelings of helplessness and the sense of loss of control.

We also learned from monitoring community interactions since September 11th that this form of suffering can bring a community closer together. Interactions have been improved by the connections made by the students and adults during this time of struggle. Whether a person was adult or student, American or Saudi, local resident or Academy community member was less important than the fact that terrorism affects virtually all people negatively. This is true because people are far more similar than not. Subsequent to the terrorist acts, some of the barriers that tend to be socially constructed were dropped or relaxed, enabling better and more profound types of communications to go on. I suspect we witnessed and participated in a more raw and genuine form of existence as a community than is typically experienced. We dealt with each other as people first.

Even with the intervention efforts, a significant downside is starting to be seen, however. Following these events, a higher than average number of our students are going back home to finish their high school experiences. Although it is disappointing for our school to lose these students, we appreciate that their physical safety, and emotional needs may have to be met among their families. Abraham Maslow's hierarchical theory of needs seems as viable today as ever. Our Saudi visitor's family did make it to the Academy and lifetime friendships are being forged in the wake of tragedy. Let us attempt to see through the social conventions that keep us apart. As this tragedy taught us, dealing with all people as human beings first, then applying appropriate counseling services based on the needs of the individual hold great promise for guiding the social and emotional development of gifted students.

For Discussion

- As a teacher or counselor, did your experiences of helping children following the September 11th tragedy mirror those of the children at the Academy? If not, how was it different?

- As a teacher and/or parent, are the school services available to deal with tragedies appropriate for the needs of gifted students?

Gifted Children Today

A recurring theme in my efforts to learn more about gifted children is how different are the times in which they are growing up from my own experience. As I have tried to evaluate their behavior and their social and emotional needs, it comes up again and again. AIDS, MTV, guns in school, the Internet—all of these impact the lives of gifted children.

I begin to explore these ideas in "Gifted Students' Social and Emotional Development in the 21st Century." Rollo May's notion that we cannot truly understand something until we have experienced it serves as a reminder to us all that we must delve ever more deeply into the psyche of young people if we want to help them succeed in these new, very different times.

In "Technology and the Unseen World of Gifted Students," I explore the use of computers with gifted students. Using Erikson's theory of psychosocial development, I also consider how engaging in various communication technologies could positively affect a gifted child's identity.

The chapters that follow also deal with many realities of gifted students' lives. The tragic incident at Columbine High School in April of 1999 is a most potent indicator of the different times in which these children are growing up. How giftedness plays a role in their experience is the emphasis of the chapter titled "The Lived Experiences of Gifted Students in School, or On Gifted Students and Columbine." Building on the concepts discussed in the first section ("About Gifted Children:

Who They Are and Why"), this chapter explores misconceptions about gifted children and how they interact with these new times to make an even more complicated world for gifted young people.

In "The Rage of Gifted Students," I examine the various layers of influence on gifted students' experiences and the ways these influences may generate feelings of rage in these individuals. I conclude this chapter with suggestions for how we can help gifted students reduce or eliminate their feelings of rage.

Another aspect of the social milieu of schools is discussed in "The Many Faces of Bullies." Gifted students are growing up in a world filled with many real and perceived threats to their physical and social safely. Appreciating the historical context in which gifted students live is an important step in guiding their social and emotional development.

The final chapter in this section, "Psychological Autopsy Provides Insight Into Gifted Adolescent Suicide," was created from my research into gifted adolescent suicide. This chapter is a synopsis of the findings of a study my colleagues, Robert Cook and David Dixon, and I conducted on the lives of three adolescents who committed suicide. The detailed description of these adolescents and their circumstances were developed through a psychological autopsy process. Learning about these students led us to the development of specific recommendations for preventing suicides of gifted adolescents. I cannot emphasize enough the need to be on the lookout for indicators of suicidal behavior and the need to be proactive, no matter how uncomfortable it may be. Professional counselors are key in the solution to the destructive notions these adolescents hold, but they can do nothing if adults are not aware of the need for their intervention.

Gifted Students' Social and Emotional Development in the 21st Century

Key Concepts

- Generational influences on psychosocial development
- To know something, one must experience it (Rollo May)
- Global economy influence on psychosocial development

The complications involved in raising children increased significantly during the second half of the 20th century. Charles Dickens' quote "It was the best of times, it was the worst of times" seems an apt statement to describe the societal changes since 1960. These changes have been so dramatic and pervasive that they are, in fact, hard to fully comprehend. The last 40 years have seen many changes, from what were once considered global issues, such as population growth and environmental concerns (seemingly so distant and unrelated to us living in the United States 40 years ago), to the daily activities in which we each engage. As we guide the youth of today, we must consider both the broad and specific contexts of our children's times. In the last 40 years, we have moved from only three available television channels to literally hundreds, from curable types of venereal diseases to herpes and AIDS, from 16k of computer memory to terabytes at roughly the same cost, letter writing to e-mail, and the world's population has grown from three billion to six billion people.

Given the important ways in which our world has changed and will continue to change, those of us from earlier generations need to appreciate that we can only know *about* what it is like to be growing up gifted in the new millennium. Despite the breadth and depth of the changes, one might argue that small-town life has not changed much over the past 40 years. While this can be a true statement, I would note that MTV is one example of how a generation has been connected through image and sound unlike all previous generations. This one simple example brings to bear all the considerations associated with psychosocial development. For example, historically, as a young child moved from parents being the ones with the greatest influence on his or her immediate behavior to friends being more influential, the small groups of friends tended to carefully reflect the child's immediate communities in terms of values, appearance, and comportment. Via MTV and other similar channels, young people of today make a visual and auditory connection with youth throughout the United States. Consequently, the reference groups of youth are no longer so closely tied to immediate communities. Issues such as fitting in, developing a peer group, understanding one's role in his or her family and the broader culture are but a few of the issues that emerge as potentially influencing the needs of gifted children. All these concerns and experiences occur as children are forming their identities.

The following are two examples of ways that children's experiences vary significantly from previous generations and illustrate meaningful variations within the past 20 years.

Schooling Practices
- from textbooks and worksheets to computers
- from teacher-directed to students as teachers
- from lecturing to students becoming responsible for the construction of their own learning through processes of inquiry

Access to Information
- from slow and sometimes unattainable to immediate and overwhelming
- from being out in the world collecting information to collecting information from home
- from collecting information manually to relying on computers

As adults, we must realize that, while we try to understand our children's lives, in many important ways they are unlike our own. A famous psychologist, Rollo May (1969), wrote that we must recognize the difference between knowing about something and truly knowing something. May described how he came down with tuberculosis and was on his deathbed. He dealt with the salient aspects and issues of preparing for death. He recovered and came to realize that, before this experience, he only knew about death. After having experienced the life of a dying person, he truly knew death. To know something, one must experience it. Most of our lives are spent merely knowing about things. As newborns, we learn in a prelingual manner largely determined by our parents until our mobility allows for our own experimentation. Even with trial and error experiences, we are being taught to learn vicariously by watching and listening to others. We also learn how to create and understand the world as mental activities without relying on others' input or examples.

Much of what we come to know about and believe comes from our environmental teachings and mental constructions, and far less through our own experiments. This distinction is important for many reasons. The first is that no two people can have the exact same understanding of any situation or construct. Another is that historical analysis has taught us that cohorts in history often reveal patterns of thought and value formations that are similar. For example, in the United States, the young adult population living during the Watergate scandal has maintained a level and type of political skepticism different from the young adults of the Reagan era. A third is that, along with the acceleration of technological advances over the past 40 years, there has been tremendous growth in the knowledge of virtually all subjects. Various means, such as the Internet and personal computers, now provide access to the expanding information base in increasingly easier and faster ways. There now exists a "digital divide," a serious and expanding gap between the knowledge, opportunities, and wealth of those in the world who have regular and easy access and those who have neither. The relationship between young children's access to self-selected material and their social and emotional development has yet to be studied. Therefore, it is difficult to predict the effects on typical development patterns of the immediate access to and consumption of material that cuts across topics and age appropriateness.

Another major confluence of events that are radically changing current experiences (and hence all that is affected by them) is the movement to a world economy. Opportunities and expectations are becoming influenced by what is and is not perceived as possible. For example, many

Indiana natives who grew up between the 1950s and the 1980s aspired to and relied on manufacturing jobs upon graduation from high school. This possibility allowed families to remain physically close and often work together. In recent years, however, the move to a world economy has drained the manufacturing jobs that defined the state's economy. Despite the fact that the state has relatively low unemployment rates of 4–5%, the adult population is often underemployed and earns a fourth to a third of previous incomes, while their children grapple with giving up on their aspirations. This evolution is slow and often painful. More importantly, these changes are being played out on a world stage where being a consumer is characterized as being a good citizen.

As concerned adults interested in helping the psychosocial development of gifted students, we should first heed Rollo May's words: To truly know and understand another's experiences, we must live them ourselves. Secondly, we should maintain a healthy respect for those experiences that are consistent across generations and those that are not. We must be aware of the differences in children's experiences and in our own. With our new appreciation for the profound differences of experience as compared to our children, we should draw on all resources available to assist the children in question. It would also be helpful for adults to learn some basic theory about human development, particularly as it pertains to the psychosocial development of gifted students. There are certain aspects of human development theory that are resistant to change over time.

By realizing our limitations in being truly empathetic and by utilizing the strategies noted, we have the opportunity to provide effective guidance to the gifted youth of the 21st century. I am sure that Rollo May, by asking us to experience another's suffering in order to know it, never meant to encourage the pain and suffering of even one additional person in order to widen expertise in the face of any specific tragedy. I am quite confident that he would have advised us to operate in a climate of trust and with an appreciation for the child's experiences as being meaningful and valid. Our role should, therefore, be one of compassion and respect for the uniqueness of all gifted children as they struggle with the development of their identity while on the path to self-actualization.

For Discussion

- Provide two further examples of how today's gifted children's experiences differ from previous generations.

- What strategies (as mentioned in previous chapters) do you think would be most effective in dealing with generational or global influences on gifted individuals' psychological development?

Technology
and the Unseen
World of
Gifted Students

Key Concepts

- Gifted students' experiences with computer-based communications technologies
- Experiences fall into four categories: freedom of expression, control, power, and feeling connected
- Erikson's theory of psychosocial development
- The positive influences of technology on Eriksonian crises

The social and emotional development of gifted students can be influenced by many factors. Genetics, experiences, learning, family values, perceptions, and interactions all contribute to the development of gifted children. Under the heading of experiences is students' use of computers. This chapter will highlight some of the most common and some of the least well-known uses of computers by gifted students. The potential effects of using these technologies will be discussed using two stages of Erikson's theory of Psychosocial Development as a framework.

For almost two decades, children have had increasing opportunities to use computers. Many homes have one or more computers, and virtually all schools in the United States have at least one. It is common for schools to have one or more computer labs. For example, the Indiana Academy for Science, Mathematics, and Humanities will be providing every student a laptop computer with wireless Internet access. Student access to personal computers has clearly been enhanced over the past 20 years.

Times have also changed in terms of the nature of the personal computers to which students have access. From the early days (circa 1982) of home computers with 16k of memory and no hard drive, to today with the 1.25 gigahertz dual processors and numerous inexpensive, yet powerful peripherals, technology has changed. The evolution in the technological capacity of computers parallels the growing options available to students. For example, just imagine the difference between the original game of *Pong* and the newer strategy game called *Deus Ex*. A similar evolution of opportunity and impact on students exists as the Internet has evolved. After word processing, the first and most common use of computers has been electronic mail (e-mail). Gaming is also very popular among children.

When trying to understand the development of our gifted children interfacing with computer-based communication technologies, we can only speculate. At this point in history, very little research exists that attempts to address the questions listed below. Consequently, this chapter is based more on my observations and experiences running a residential high school for academically gifted students and, to a small degree, involvement with my own children.

Four Types of Communications Technologies

E-Mail

People of all ages and backgrounds use e-mail to communicate with others. Issues associated with time and distance are easily surpassed using this technology. Messages are sent with or without attachments. Pictures and even full-motion video can be passed from one to another around the world requiring very little time. For example, a baby can be born in Houston, TX, at 3 a.m., and moments later grandparents in Hawaii can download and print pictures of the newborn child. These opportunities, while recent to adults (over the past 20 years), are common to the children of today. This fact means that our children are growing up with greater facility with computer-based technologies than their parents, a fact that should not be underappreciated.

Instant Messaging

Instant messaging, in some ways a more limited form of e-mail, is quite common today, with students communicating with multiple "buddies" at one time in real time. Because of technological enhancements, these interactions go on while other computer activities are being carried out. It is similar to being on the telephone, but with many people at once. Increasingly, students use this communications technology while doing homework. In essence, gifted students separated by varying distances communicate while engaging in other activities.

Chat Rooms

Chat rooms tend to be made up of people with some interest in common. They communicate often without knowing the other people with whom they are "chatting." The chat rooms range from being relatively public to being extremely private. One's involvement may be a single event, a regular pattern, or an ongoing compulsion.

Online Diaries or Journals

The final example is online diaries or journals, which are less common than the previous examples. Online journals take many forms. Some are relatively confidential, with only chosen outsiders able to view the materials. At the opposite end of the continuum are journals open to everyone. Details revealed using this form of communication run the gamut from relatively innocuous information to descriptions of the most personal kind.

Erikson's Theory of Psychosocial Development

Before highlighting salient parts of the experience of engaging people through these forms of technology, I want to use Erik Erikson's (1963) theory of Psychosocial Development to provide some parameters. His theory is important because it establishes a framework for understanding the typical psychosocial developmental patterns of people. A second important feature of Erikson's theory is its claim that a person's id is free from internal conflict, but susceptible in its development to psychosocial conflict, not internal psychosexual conflict as Freud had claimed. Erikson believed that conflict arises from a person's interaction with his or her environment, not merely the internal forces of the person. Consequently, the culture in which a person lives is important to his or her psychosocial development, a position I have espoused for 20 years.

Erikson's theory includes eight developmental stages. During each stage, a crisis must be resolved in order for a person to develop without carrying forward issues tied to the previous crises. During the infancy stage (first year of life), Erikson posits that the primary crisis to be resolved is one of trust vs. mistrust. He described the task to be resolved during the second year of life (toddler) as autonomy vs. shame and doubt. The preschooler stage (years 3–5) includes initiative vs. guilt as the primary crisis. Elementary school stage includes competence vs. inferiority as the crisis to be resolved. Adolescence is the period when the individual must refine his or her sense of identity or struggle with role confusion. During early adulthood, intimacy vs. isolation is the crisis to be resolved. Generativity or despair is the crisis to be resolved during middle adulthood. The final developmental crisis was called integrity vs. despair.

According to Erikson, as the individual negotiates a crisis at each stage of development, a basic strength or virtue emerges. He described eight basic virtues that he believed emerge across a person's psychosocial development: hope, will, purpose, competence, fidelity, love, care, and wisdom, respectively. Because this chapter focuses on school-aged children, only the third (competence vs. inferiority) and fourth (identity vs. role confusion) psychosocial crises will be discussed.

Experiences and Benefits

The following is a list of experiences and benefits that I feel comfortable reporting as part of using computer-based communications technologies. Generally speaking, the experience of using e-mail, instant messaging, chat rooms, and online diaries falls into four major categories: freedom of expression, control, power, and feeling connected. Each of these four also contains nuances that vary across people. For example, for some gifted students, freedom of expression includes a greater sense of empowerment rooted in the immediacy and control of the expression; it can also serve as a catharsis. Others experience feelings of excitement and joy to have convenient outlets for expression when they perceive that much of their lives are controlled by adults (parents and teachers). Remaining anonymous when communicating can create feelings of safety and power. Crossing age groups often creates feelings of being adult-like, as well as a sense of rebelliousness. Other feelings associated with using these forms of technologies include privacy, immediacy, ownership, imagination, freedom, utility, and feeling the belonging that comes from participating with others of similar interest. Perhaps the greatest experience that comes from these forms of interaction is a greater sense of connectedness and, therefore, acceptance. Many gifted children have commented on their surprise at finding other people "like me."

With the experiences and benefits possible from using these forms of computer-based communications technologies, what are the ramifications for the social and emotional development of gifted students relative to Erikson's third (competence vs. inferiority) and fourth (identity vs. role confusion) crises of development? While it is too early to tell and there is far too little research currently available, we can say that we are immersed in a culture wherein these kinds of interactions are increasingly common to our young gifted population. It is reasonable to assume that these behaviors will increase to the point where future generations of gifted students have a large portion of their relationships created in this virtual world. It is easy to see positive potential in the development of competence in the use of these technologies. For example, communicating with others via technology requires a modest degree of skill. Typing, navigating the Internet, word processing, composing, analyzing, and generally expressing one's thoughts and feelings are skills that can be enhanced using these forms of communication. All these examples are indicative of skills that can lead to an increasing sense of agency and positive self-concept.

We can imagine how the positive experiences and benefits of engaging in these communication technologies could positively affect a gifted child's identity. Having outlets for expression that allow for valued interactions with others that provide information and build relationships are important aspects to the development of one's identity. Arguably, the most important benefit of using computer-based communications to interact with others is the feeling of being connected (part of a community) and gaining a sense of belonging. From those feelings, acceptance is often the next step of development to emerge. It is very important in the lives of gifted students to feel accepted. This allows them to move forward in life not feeling aberrant or detached from society. Moreover, as Erikson described in his theory, several virtues can develop as the crises are resolved. The virtues he proposes are, therefore, potentially tied to the benefits of the students' use of these communications technologies. The outlined experiences and benefits can assist in resolving the crises at the two stages of development discussed, potentially influencing the emergence of the virtues of hope, will, purpose, and competence.

If these Eriksonian crises can be positively affected by the use of these technologies, why do adults carry around so much worry and concern about (gifted) children using them? There are several reasons for this. Most adults did not grow up with access to computers and therefore do not have the facility for, and comfort level with, using them in this manner. A second reason is that the adults' role in the children's upbringing can seem diminished when they cannot participate with the children. There is a great fear of the unknown, and due to the media's portrayal of children being exploited at the hands of the unscrupulous, adults' worries are enhanced. In a nutshell, adults' unfamiliarity causes them to feel cautious and somewhat impotent.

Unanswered Questions

The social and emotional development of gifted children is clearly being affected by the use of these communication technologies. How they are being affected is only now beginning to emerge. Below I have listed numerous unanswered questions about how the use of these computer-based communications technologies affects gifted students' social and emotional development.

- What are the effects on the social and emotional development of gifted students of brief encounters with others they do not see? For example, what are the effects on their identity formation, friendship formation, and issues of self?
- What are the effects of short- and long-term interactions when anonymity is ever-present among some or all of the participants?

- What are the effects of new relationships and friendships emerging from these modes of communication?
- How does building relationships using these technologies translate back into school?
- How does building relationships using these technologies affect the third (competence vs. inferiority) and fourth (identity vs. role confusion) crises of Erikson's theory?
- What direction can be provided to adults about the use of communications technologies in raising and teaching gifted students?

As with most aspects of guiding the social and emotional development of gifted students, until these questions are answered, it is important that we stay involved with our children and use common sense about setting limitations and providing safety for them. We also need to support our children's interests and learn about them to the extent that we can. Having faith in them, while at the same time realizing that they are children, is always good advice. And, some time in the near future, answers to these questions will provide additional guidance for us as we attempt to guide our gifted students' social and emotional development.

For Discussion

A number of unanswered questions were put forward. Select and discuss a question that you consider important:

- What are the effects on the social and emotional development of gifted students of brief encounters with others they do not see? For example, what are the effects on their identity formation, friendship formation, and issues of self?

- What are the effects of short- and long-term interactions when anonymity is ever-present among some or all of the participants?

- What are the effects of new relationships and friendships emerging from these modes of communication?

- How does building relationships using these technologies translate back into school?

- How does building relationships using these technologies affect the third (competence vs. inferiority) and fourth (identity vs. role confusion) crises of Erikson's theory?

- What direction can be provided to adults about the use of communications technologies in raising and teaching gifted students?

The Lived Experiences of Gifted Students in School, or On Gifted Students and Columbine

---

Key Concepts

- Stigma of Giftedness Paradigm
- Idiosyncratic patterns of development
- Gifted students deal with mixed messages at a micro level and macro level in school.

The purpose of this chapter is to create a context for understanding gifted students' lives in school. To that end, I will highlight how gifted students deal with the mixed messages they perceive from their environment and try to make a connection with the tragedy at Columbine High School. While the topic is quite somber, there is ultimately good news to be shared about gifted students' lives.

Since the middle 1980s, Larry Coleman, and I have been publishing research about the lives of gifted students in school (e.g., Coleman & Cross, 1988; Cross, Coleman, & Terhaar-Yonkers, 1991). Data for some of the early articles published on this topic were collected during evaluations of schools and programs for gifted students. During the early evaluations (circa 1984), the gifted students described in great detail what their lives in their local schools were "really like." The "really like" aspect of their comments inspired us to approach the research in a more serious, deliberate, and focused manner. Since then Larry and I, individually and in tandem, have gathered data from thousands of gifted students in grades K–12 from numerous states across the nation. We have used surveys and questionnaires; made observations; interviewed students, teachers, parents, and administrators; visited numerous schools and classrooms; and read students' journals all in the quest of understanding gifted students' lives in school. Over the past 15 years, we have published approximately 20 articles and presented more than 40 papers together at conferences dealing with gifted students. The research has led me to my ideas about the shootings at Columbine. This chapter will provide ideas that were developed while working on the various studies previously reported. In addition to this line of research, I have increasingly focused on the psychology of gifted students, with a specialization in the suicidal behaviors of gifted students. Our research into the social and emotional development of gifted students, their experiences of giftedness, their social cognition, and their social coping strategies and behaviors have also informed this chapter.

For 20 years, I have claimed that schools are first and foremost a social enterprise where some academic learning goes on. While I have used this statement to frame my social-cognitive orientation, the original idea emerged during an interview with a gifted adolescent who was describing to me his life as a student. The detail reflected in his perceptions about the expectations within his numerous school placements was most impressive. He also described expectations from outside his school that reflect messages society held about gifted students. The degree to which the messages were mixed was quite astonishing to me. For example, he perceived that gifted students are physically weak, socially inadequate, and not interesting people. They are out of touch, unattractive, and have a high propensity for mental problems. While the student knew that many of these descriptors did not fit him, he had come to believe that being gifted was somewhat limiting. Another important message he received was that going to college was important. To go to college, one needs to work hard as a student. He also believed that pursuing excellence was important in life. For example, "do your best" was described as the single most frequent comment from adults. Across these various messages was a thread that established implicit parameters on his behavior that was different than the messages. The thread was interpreted as *not too*. Study hard, but *not too* hard. Pursue academic passions, but *not too* much. Even do your best in school, but *not* if it means spending *too* much time or energy to do so. Increasingly, the understood message was that, to be a healthy person, one spreads time spent in activities across a variety of endeavors that seem reasonable to adults. A secondary message inferred from these mixed messages was that being gifted should not take so much of your time or, said differently, if one must spend so much time on his or her academic studies, then he or she must not be gifted.

Over the years, I have heard other beliefs held by many gifted students that pertain to these mixed messages. Three of the most common are that others hold expectations about gifted students; that if one becomes known as a gifted student, it affects how others treat him or her; and that one learns that if he or she can manage the information others gain about him or her, then he or she can maintain a more social latitude. This information management system becomes the means gifted students use to navigate the social expectations and the mixed messages society holds about them. These three beliefs are called the Stigma of Giftedness Paradigm (SGP; Coleman, 1985). The SGP has been studied for years and found to be a good way to understand and explain gifted students' experience in school settings. The social cognition and coping strategies are also explained by this understanding of the basic SGP.

Recently, some important writings have attempted to compare and contrast the developmental patterns of gifted students by comparing them to patterns of typical development. Some of the more idiosyncratic patterns of development are also being explored. By the latter, I mean the development of gifted students that reflects their own emerging biologically determined qualities, natural developmental tendencies, environmental opportunities, their own agency, and specific opportunities to develop in areas not typical for others. This area of study will require decades of exploration. For now, I think that, in order to understand the lives of gifted students, it is important to note one's time in history, large societal influences, more localized social expectations, and specific patterns of influence on gifted children.

An important finding in an early study was that young gifted students perceive expectations and societal messages through the eyes of an immature mind. Because their social and emotional development is often more age-appropriate than their academic abilities, consideration of the early perceptions of mixed messages on their development needs serious ongoing study.

What can we say about gifted students' experiences in school? They receive mixed messages. Some messages are at the macro level, while others are at the micro level. Others are internal to the individual. They try to understand and live within the messages they receive. They develop social-coping strategies to blend in with their environments to the extent they desire. Gifted students experience the same societal influences as their cohort. For example, access to weapons, suicidal patterns, and familial problems or issues (e.g., divorce rates) also impact them. All these influences are also affected by friendships and idiosyncratic qualities of the individual. For example, an individual's level of mental health is a key ingredient to both his or her experiences in school and his or her behaviors.

All these influences bring us to the shootings of students at Columbine High School in Littleton, CO. Before I comment specifically on that event, I want to add to the equation a few other influences that were important, yet rarely discussed. All students are forced by law to be in the presence of other students for several hours a day in close proximity. Teachers typically have their time dedicated to specific tasks that direct their time and energy to certain settings. What emerge are behaviors from the students that society either allows or does not actively discourage. For example, some adults assume that, in school, students bully each other and girls need to learn how to be able to turn away those who harass them. From a sociological perspective, I assert that a society's prejudices are allowed to exist within schools. Racism, sexism, classism, and so forth are present and active in most schools. The fact that these exist in school is not meant to be a criticism of teachers. I have a great deal of respect for teachers as the individuals who often end or prevent these problems. We can take as an example of the rampant prejudice held by students a group that has for years been subjected to numerous types of assaults: gay and lesbian students. This group illustrate how difficult it is to exist in these microcosms of society we call schools. When the mixed messages that gifted students experience are factored in with the extent to which other prejudices manifest themselves in schools, it is quite amazing to me that gifted kids tend to be as well adjusted as they are.

Several parents of gifted students have told me that their children have surprised them by saying that, while they do not condone the shooting of other students at Columbine, they can understand the feelings of rage that go along with being tormented in school. These parents drew on their own experiences to conclude that trials and tribulations—vis-à-vis bullying and harassment—of students today are the same as those they had as children. Students' experiences in school today are somewhat similar to and somewhat different from the experiences of previous generations. How they are the same is important, and how they are different is very important. Children should feel safe while in school. They cannot thrive when they feel threatened. They grow up in environments knowing anyone who gets mad at them can easily access a gun. Their antagonist may even have the gun with them while at school. Even those few people from previous generations who did have similar worries would not have had to seriously consider the possibility of contending with automatic weapons or pipe bombs.

The final factor I believe to be pertinent to the lived experience of gifted students is that the beliefs learned adults hold about gifted students are often tacit to them. They only come to realize what they believe when faced with events or circumstances that bring to the surface their actual beliefs or feelings. For example, a few years ago a sophisticated reporter for the *Chicago Tribune* interviewed me about Theodore Kaczynski, the "Unabomber." The reporter had worked for weeks putting together a story about Kaczynski's history that emphasized the fact that he was a gifted student. Several leaders in the field of gifted education were interviewed. The reporter asked me, "Did Ted Kaczynski commit murder because he was allowed to skip two grades in school?" What an amazing assumption! Does accelerating gifted students cause them to become serial killers? My response was, "I hope not, because tens of thousands of students are grade-skipped each year." I was stunned to learn that such an educated person could hold such foolish misconceptions. Imagine what messages are sent to gifted students by less well-educated or academically oriented people. Also imagine how gifted students are actually treated if large numbers of adults, including well-educated adults, hold such wild misconceptions about them.

Putting the Pieces Together

Gifted students need adults to guide them. They need adults who understand them to help them develop with few limitations. Although patterns and trends among people can be understood at the macro level, acts of individuals must be understood at the individual level. The students at Columbine who murdered their classmates have been described in the press as gifted students. The lesson of Columbine is not that gifted students are homicidal; rather, the lesson is that the children who killed other students had certain qualities, histories, and experiences. They had access to lethal weapons and the time to plan the killings. Their giftedness should in no way be assumed as a cause agent in their inappropriate act. Their behavior has become a mirror for society's prejudice. A lesson of Columbine should be that schools must create safe environments where learning can thrive. Larger issues like the relationship between the size of schools and the social milieu should be considered. Our research has suggested that being gifted in differing types of school settings leads to different experiences.

Another important question should be, "What size or configuration of school allows for optimal relationships to be forged among students, between students and teachers, and students and guidance counselors?" Few professionals who work in or with public schools believe that we are able to create optimal educational settings. We seem destined to work with what we have. For example, some high schools are so large that their school counselors rarely get to know the students for whom they are responsible. In Indiana, the ratio of high school students to school counselors often exceeds 400 to 1. This speaks to the extent to which schools are not effectively designed to prevent incidents like the one at Columbine. Rather than finding easy, quick condemnations for gifted students, we must commit ourselves to helping all students thrive, including gifted students.

Looking for ways to create positive environments in which all of these students can coexist and actually thrive should be a goal of our society. Blaming schools, television violence, video violence, or divorce rates for the events at Columbine are superficial and will only lead to band-aid approaches to long-term complicated problems. While I am troubled about the deaths of the victims at Columbine, I am hoping that Americans will recognize that our culture tolerates the abuse of disempowered students to such a degree that it requires a rare event to bring it to the surface.

For Discussion

- Was the Columbine incident a catalyst for change in your school?

- Comment on the question stated in the chapter: What size or configuration of school allows for optimal relationships to be forged among students and guidance counselors?

The Rage
of Gifted Students

Key Concepts

- Brofenbrenner's ecological approach to contexts of development
- Gifted students and the influence of macrosystems, exosystems, mesosystems, and microsystems on their lives
- Social milieus in schools and the idiosyncratic patterns of effects on a gifted student's development

---

The experiences of gifted students in school are quite varied and reflect a wide variety of factors. For 17 years, I have written about their experiences from two perspectives, that of a researcher and, using their own words, that of the students themselves. I have come to believe that the lived experiences, or *Lebensvelt*, of gifted students in school is one of the richest areas in the field of gifted education in which to conduct research.

I believe that we are far from understanding the relationship between the experiences of gifted students, how they make sense of these experiences, and how these experiences affect gifted students' behaviors in school and their long-term psychological development. As our society has evolved, our schools increasingly have become a setting where all of society's values interact. Our beliefs, hopes, aspirations, and prejudices coexist in tight physical quarters. Some schools, such as a new $74 million high school in Indiana, provide students with beautiful surroundings and state-of-the-art equipment. Other schools, as so eloquently documented by Jonathan Kozol (1991), are disgraceful, run-down facilities, struggling to provide their students such basic necessities as textbooks. Schools exist in the largest cities and the smallest towns. All schools have two things in common—policymakers rely on them to acculturate students into the preferred mold, and it is expected that this will be done for the least amount of money possible. All of the children from age 5 or 6 attend because it is the law. In all these various settings, parents hope that their children's lives will be improved by earning a good education.

All these factors and circumstances exist within a large system of dominant beliefs and ideologies that Bronfenbrenner (1994) described in his ecological approach to contexts of development as a macrosystem. The *macrosystem* is the larger context of values and mores that influence the behaviors of the students. The next system, the *exosystem*, includes linkages between two or more settings that affect the individual. Mass media, governmental agencies, educational systems, and religious hierarchy may impact the individual indirectly. The *mesosystem* is where the various microsystems interact. The individual lives daily in the *microsystem* of school, home, and neighborhood. For example, a gifted adolescent lives with his or her family and attends a local school (microsystem), may see his or her school friends in church or in the neighborhood (mesosystem), learns from the mass media about stereotypes he or she should hold (exosystem), all within the framework of Christian capitalism, the dominant ideology of our country (macrosystem). The public schools in the United States have been described as anti-intellectual environment (Howley, Howley, & Pendarvis, 1995), an attitude promoted in the exosystem, dealt with directly in the mesosystem and perhaps causing conflict daily in the microsystem.

These various layers of influence on gifted students' experiences cut across their values and cause them to look for meaning in those experiences. Gifted students often receive mixed messages from the ideas and values represented in the exo- and mesosystems. Common mixed messages that older gifted students experience include claims by some adults that giftedness does not exist, does not matter, or that gifted students are already advantaged and should not receive any special consideration.

Parents encourage them to do well in school, while at the same time, students describe their experiences in school primarily as being bored, and waiting for other students to catch up. Perceptions of how they are valued in their school, how students and adults treat them, are created and internalized, sometimes leading to feelings of rage. According to the *Webster's College Dictionary* (Costello, 1992), one definition for rage is "a violent desire or passion."(p. 1113) While very few gifted students act-out in violent ways, many do seem to acknowledge internalized feeling of rage. This column will attempt to articulate what I believe is a deep-seated rage that many gifted students feel. I will note how I came to this conclusion and a few ideas about what we might be able to do to improve the situation.

Throughout my career, I have observed, interviewed, counseled, and tested gifted students. To date, I have accumulated data from approximately a dozen states and 15,000 gifted students. Much of these data have come from school and program evaluations that I have conducted. My professional interest has always been to try to capture the essence of their experiences and to eventually create a model of development representing their stories. A belief I have come to hold is that gifted students are affected by their experiences in differing school settings in individual ways. For example, in small rural schools, students describe the experience of being gifted as being part of a family or community. On the other hand, students in large suburban schools describe feelings of being stereotyped with limited social latitude. A function of this experience is often to maintain the social status one has by playing a role—in this case, the stereotypical gifted student. Avoiding threats to the role status becomes a priority, leading students to avoid taking positive risks and to create social-coping strategies. Tacit-coping strategies are also formed. In essence, the social milieu of each school is different, causing idiosyncratic patterns of effects on a student's development.

The media reported several incidents of homicide in high schools in the 1990s. "Reported" is an understatement. The stories were broadcast over and over and over. Perhaps the most dramatic of these tragedies occurred at Columbine High School in Littleton, CO. The news portrayed the events hourly for weeks after the event. The lesson we took away was that our children are not safe in school, and there was an (implied) additional threat from gifted students. The lessons we should have learned were that our children's experiences in high school (middle and elementary school) cause them to suffer. After the events at

Columbine, I interviewed dozens of adolescent, gifted students about the event. Without one exception they stated that what the killers did was wrong and unforgivable, but, those I interviewed, all knew how they felt. They knew how the killers felt. I was quite taken by this. Adults were acting flabbergasted, looking for every conceivable explanation for the murders: video games, access to weaponry, and giftedness. I have since gone back and reread samples of transcripts and tape recordings of dozens of interviews I conducted over the past 15 years, and I was dismayed to find that the same thread was often conveyed. Because no tragic events were at the front of the minds of the gifted students being interviewed, I had phrased my questions in ways that did not encourage this type of evidence to appear as directly as in the post-Columbine interviews. But, in one way or another, many of the gifted students provided evidence of feeling rage about their treatment.

One of my former gifted students who had returned to his alma mater to build a Beowulf system of multiple computers, showed me an Internet Web site (http://slashdot.org/articles/99/04/25/1438249.shtml) made up of approximately 30 pages of adults' and high school students' comments about their high school experience. Jon Katz (2001) serialized the comments into the "Voices From the Hellmouth" series. Many of the hundreds of contributors nationwide self-reported being gifted students. Their rage is palpable. Below is the quote of one contributor to this serial.

"I stood up in social studies class—the teacher wanted a discussion, and said I could never kill anyone or condone anyone who did kill anyone. But I could, on some level, understand these kids in Colorado, the killers. Because day after day, slight after slight, exclusion after exclusion, you can learn how to hate, and that hatred grows and takes you over sometimes, especially when you come to see that you're hated only because you're smart and different, or sometimes even because you are on-line a lot, which is still so uncool to many kids? After class, I was called to the principal's office and told that I had to agree to undergo five sessions of counseling or be expelled from school, as I had expressed sympathy with the killers in Colorado, and the school had to be able to explain itself if I acted out. In other words, for speaking freely, and to cover their ass, I was not only branded a weird geek, but a potential killer. That will sure help deal with violence in America." Jay (Original Comment #1)

How widespread is this problem? Unfortunately I cannot answer this question. I do believe that it exists and to a much greater degree that adults know.

What can we do to help gifted students reduce or eliminate their feeling of rage? How much of this is normal teen angst? Turn of the century psychologist G. Stanley Hall (1904) described adolescence as a period of "storm and stress." His work, along with that of other psychodynamic psychologists, created widespread belief that adolescents necessarily go through these periods. More recent developmental psychologists have largely discredited these claims. Many espouse the belief that some adolescents have this conflict-ridden experience of adolescence, while others only experience the conflict episodically. Many do not experience adolescence as a difficult period at all (Offer & Offer, 1975). My contention is that the mixed messages that gifted students receive across the various systems that Bronfenbrenner (1994) outlined, along with normal developmental issues, plus the repetitious images of adolescents engaging in homicides, suicides, and other undesirable behavior all contribute to the rage. Unfortunately, because adults had some undesirable experiences while in school, they believe that what gifted students experience is just the same rite of passage that they endured. While I have little doubt that some of the current experiences gifted students are having would fit that category, I contend that contemporary gifted students experience taunting, bullying, and generalized, threatening behavior in ways different than in the past. The media has created beliefs in the minds of our students that they are not safe in schools.

The first step toward helping these students is to acknowledge that their experiences are not exactly the same as ours. Another is to work with the schools to bring about nonthreatening environments that do not tolerate any taunting or bullying. A next level of improvement is the need to work toward consistent messages being sent to gifted students about their value, worth, and responsibilities. The last suggestion cuts across most levels of Bronfenbrenner's model. Therefore, families and teachers will need to try to bring about change locally. Because the greatest influence will likely come from the individual and microsystem, beginning there makes the most sense. Disallowing negative remarks, anti-intellectual behavior, and encouraging respect for individuals of all ability levels and interests can be done and almost certainly will improve the conditions of all students in school.

For Discussion

- How would you respond if someone made the comment that feelings of rage in students is normal teen angst?

- What can families and teachers do to bring about change at the local level to improve conditions for gifted children?

The Many Faces of Bullies

Key Concepts

- Broadening definitions of bullies
- Perceived threats in the lives of gifted students

Gifted students today experience many disruptions in their lives. Some of these disruptions are relatively unique to them, for example, needing to hide how well one does in school as a means to fit into an anti-intellectual school environment (Coleman & Cross, 2001). Others are believed to be common to many students, such as facing bullies.

We have all seen bullies on television shows and can even name names of bullies from our childhood days. We tend to think of bullies (for the most part) as larger than average, dull, mean-spirited males who taunt and physically push around weaker boys. Within this stereotype, one experiences an ongoing, long-term tormented relationship with another. Ironically, a romantic notion is often maintained as well—"if he just knew me, he would treat me better" or "all he needs is for one person to stand up to him and he will back down."

While examples of this stereotypical bully do exist in real life, maintaining this 1950s Hollywood depiction provides a disservice to our gifted students. According to *Webster's Dictionary* (1979), a bully is "a person who hurts, frightens, threatens, or tyrannizes over those who are smaller or weaker"(p. 240). This is a convenient definition that supports the stereotypes propagated in films and television programs. If one focuses more on the outcome of the efforts of the bullies rather than the intentions, a much broader array of people qualify as bullies of gifted students.

Let me provide a slightly different definition of a bully. A bully is a person who uses any approach at his or her disposal including, but not limited to, intimidation (physical, emotional, verbal), positional authority, relational authority, or societal authority to create limiting effects on another's behaviors, thoughts, or feelings. With this definition, one can easily see how many different people can disrupt their lives. For example, bullies can now be recognized as coming in all sizes, shapes, and from various backgrounds. They are male and female, struggling and successful students, and representing all age groups. They are accomplished at being bullies and are unaware that they are bullies. The faces of bullies are as many as are the behaviors in which they engage to disrupt the lives of others.

My observation is that the operative list of bullies with whom gifted students actually deal includes parents and other relatives, teachers, coaches, administrators, counselors, librarians, strangers, and even other gifted students. A few common examples include school administrators' claims that all kids are gifted or that no kids are gifted, and then their denial of reasonable requests to accommodate the student's learning need; a physical education teacher's criticisms of a gifted student's lack of interest in passion for, or success in athletic endeavors; a classroom teacher's discouragement of questions by gifted students or their desire to purse their academic passions. This group of bullies' common bond is the effect of their behavior on the lives of gifted students. More specifically, the bullies disrupt the normal development of gifted students by creating a perceived threat in the mind of the gifted student. In its purest form, to bully is to control.

How does this play out in the lives of gifted students? Before I address this, let us remember that our children are growing up during a time when they perceive threats all around them. My generation was raised to fear nuclear war and the Red Menace. Occasional drills were held to "protect students from nuclear attack." While the drills provided an occasional reminder that some adults were worried, the machinery to create and support a high level of chronic worry in children did not exist then as it does today. Today, there are 200 television channels, multiple competing news outlets, the Internet, and newspapers that constantly bombard children with images of threats to their survival.

As I grew older, the threat of nuclear war faded. Today's youth receive messages 24 hours a day telling them that their schools are not safe, their homes are not safe, their communities are not safe, and, on the horizon, there are numerous countries led by crazed anti-American dictators determined to end life as we know it. Added to this mix are additional messages that gifted students receive that they are aberrant (Coleman & Cross, 1988). It is within this context that our gifted students understand bullies. Local circumstances that may reveal actual physical threats to their well-being must also be considered. For example, youth in certain settings may live among gun wielding gangs, while many do not. In essence, this phenomenon combines real and merely perceived threats to both one's physical and social safety at a time in history when media outlets suggest that no one is safe.

I would like to point out one more factor in this mixture: the effectiveness of variable reinforcement schedules on human behavior. Against the gray backdrop of violence, all it takes for people to affirm their fears are occasional acts of violence. The violence can even be half a world away and still reinforce perceptions. Given this historical context in which gifted students live, how can we help guide their social and emotional development as it pertains to dealing with bullies?

- Learn a broader definition of bullying behavior.
- Realize that bullying behavior can be both intentional and unintentional.
- Learn to recognize the different ways in which one can be bullied.
- Learn strategies for dealing with the bullying behaviors.
- Test perceptions—gifted students need to learn how to approach the perceived bully about the person's actual intentions. This is especially true when dealing with teachers and other school personnel.
- Use sounding boards—gifted students need to use others as sounding boards to help them test their perceptions.
- Self-talk—gifted students need to engage in self-talk about what the actual intention of the bullying behavior is.

- Counseling—gifted students need to create a fluid counseling relationship that can provide support and problem-solving opportunities for the student. It can also help by enlisting an adult as an advocate.

Armed with these skills, gifted students can reduce the impediments to their positive development. As the primary caretakers of students with gifts and talents, let us join forces to help these students reach their potential as people.

For Discussion

- What is your definition of a bully?

- As a teacher, parent, or counselor, what steps can you take to reduce perceived threats for gifted children?

- As a teacher, parent, or counselor, discuss strategies that may be effective in dealing with bullying behaviors.

Psychological Autopsy Provides Insight Into Gifted Adolescent Suicide

---

Key Concepts

- Psychological autopsy
- Commonalities and themes emerged from study

In the chapter "Examining Claims about Gifted Children and Suicide," I mentioned a study being conducted on the suicides of three gifted adolescents. That study appeared in a special issue of *The Journal of Secondary Gifted Education* (Spring 1996, vol. 7, no. 3). This chapter will highlight the findings of the study entitled "Psychological Autopsies of Three Academically Talented Adolescents Who Committed Suicide." I hope that the information will assist in the identification of gifted students who are at risk for suicidal behavior so that a reasoned intervention can take place.

Background Information

The three adolescent males in this study had attended a state-funded, residential high school for 280 academically talented 11th- and 12th-grade students in a midwestern state.

Research Methods

The psychological autopsy was designed to assess a variety of factors, including behaviors, thoughts, feelings, and relationships of an individual who is deceased (Ebert, 1987). It was originally developed as a means of resolving equivocal deaths and has expanded to include the analysis of nonequivocal suicides, with the intention of reducing their likelihood in similar groups of people (Jones, 1977; Neill, Benensohn, Farber, & Resnick, 1974). It can be used as a posthumous evaluation of mental, social, and environmental influences on the suicide victim.

The psychological autopsy includes information from two areas: interviews with people who had significant relationships with the victim (e.g., parents, siblings, friends, teachers, romantic partners) and archival information related to the victim (e.g., school records, test information, medical records, personal letters, essays, diaries, suicide notes, artwork). Investigators analyze the information to identify themes and issues that may be valuable in the prediction of suicide within similar groups of people.

Results

The results have been organized into three categories: commonalities with adolescent suicide, commonalities among the three related to their giftedness, and themes that emerged across the three cases. The results have been excerpted with permission from the article "Psychological Autopsies of Three Academically Talented Adolescents Who Committed Suicide" by Cross, Cook, and Dixon (1996).

Commonalities With Adolescent Suicide in the General Population

1. All subjects were adolescent Caucasian males.
2. They each manifest four emotional commonalities:
    * depression,
    * anger,
    * mood swings, and
    * confusion about the future.
3. They each manifest three behavioral commonalities:

- poor impulse control,
- substance use and abuse, and
- extensive journaling.
4. They each manifest four relational commonalities:
    - romantic relationship difficulties,
    - self-esteem difficulties (either by exaggeration or self-condemnation),
    - conflictual family relationships, and
    - isolation from persons capable of disconfirming irrational logic.
5. The subjects shared warning signs in six categories:
    - behavior problems,
    - period of escalation of problems,
    - constriction (withdrawal, friends, dichotomous thinking, talk of suicide),
    - talking about suicide,
    - changes in school performance, and
    - family histories of psychological problems.

Commonalities Among the Three Cases
Related to Their Giftedness

1. The subjects exhibited overexcitabilities:
    - Expressed in ways or levels beyond the norm even among their gifted peers.
    - Had minimal prosocial outlets.
    - Experienced difficulty separating fact from fiction, especially overidentification with negative asocial or aggressive characters or themes in books and movies.
    - Experienced intense emotions.
    - Felt conflicted, pained, and confused.
    - Devalued emotional experience, except for pain.
2. They each expressed polarized, hierarchical, egocentric value systems.
3. They each engaged in group discussions of suicide as a viable and honorable solution.
4. They each expressed behavior consistent with Dabrowski's Level II or Level III of Positive Disintegration.
5. They each attended residential school as a means of escape (family, hometown).

Themes Emerging Across the Three Cases

1. All three suffered from depression: Case 1 was hospitalized for depression; Case 2 was a classic marked depression (his journal clearly reflects the depressive thought of negative view of self, negative view of the future); and Case 3 was identified as in need of treatment by school personnel, and his journal reflects clinical depression.

2. Suicide contagion seemed to have been operative: Case 3 seemed particularly to follow Case 2, while Case 1 set the stage for discussion of suicide, and the suicide of the musical group Nirvana's lead singer, Kurt Cobain, was related.

3. Suicide has a cultural component: music (e.g., Nirvana, Jane's Addiction, Sex Pistols), literature (e.g., Anne Rice, H. P. Lovecraft), and movies (e.g., *Heathers*) all played important parts for these adolescents. Even though many teenagers may consume similar media, there seemed to be an excessive focus on dark, negative content.

4. They had many characteristics identified as overexcitabilities (e.g., very sensitive, two were vegetarians, fantasy, mixing truth and fiction).

5. Suicide has a social component. The topic of suicide was openly discussed among the students in their peer groups; their discussions reduced the taboo associated with suicide and supported their position that suicide is a free choice that was their decision to make. As a result, there was no need to seek help or make referrals.

6. Excessive introspection and obsessive thinking was evident. The journals served as ways to avoid interaction with others, and, as a result, irrational thinking fed itself rather than being disconfirmed by others.

7. The issue of control over others was present in two cases. This control resulted in attempts to harm in one case.

Unanswered Questions

The following is a list of questions that remain largely unanswered at the end of the study.

1. How large a role does suicide contagion play in multiple suicides?
2. What role does unsupervised journaling play in suicide?

3. What is the extent of influence that overexcitabilities play in suicide ideation and behavior?
4. Does exploring dark issues by this age group make them vulnerable to suicide?
5. What is the effect on suicide behavior of residential schools aggregating students with similar high-risk factors (e.g., previous suicide ideation or attempts) in a setting that encourages self-exploration?
6. What role does the combination of asynchronous development and dark literature play in suicide ideation?
7. What role does the lack of religious beliefs have on suicide behavior?
8. What is the influence of popular cultural icons who commit suicide on suicide behavior of gifted adolescents?
9. What effect does believing suicide is an honorable option have on suicide behavior?
10. What is the role that popular media, where violence (including suicide and homicide) are pervasive, have on suicide behavior?

I offer these suggestions for you to consider as you think about the social and emotional needs of gifted children. You are cautioned to remember that the results were based on only three cases and, therefore, may not be representative of the larger phenomenon.

Recommendations for Preventing the Suicides of Gifted Adolescents

1. Keep an eye out for:
   - emotional difficulties, especially anger or depression;
   - lack of prosocial activities;
   - dissatisfaction with place, situation, school, peers, family, or self;
   - difficulties in romantic relationships, especially with peers of similar abilities;
   - non-normative expression of overexcitabilities, especially unbalanced expression of overexcitabilities (predominantly negative, asocial, or antisocial); and
   - difficulty separating fact from fiction (overidentification with characters, especially antiheroes and aggressive characters).

2. Err on the side of caution.
    - Do not overlook potential signs of suicide just because the child is gifted.
    - Accept the uniqueness of gifted adolescents, but not at the risk of overlooking indicators of emotional, psychological, or suicidal distress.
3. Be proactive.
    - Educate gifted adolescents about their emotional experiences and needs.
    - Communicate, communicate, communicate.
    - Challenge the idea that suicide is an honorable solution.
    - Strive for a balance of positive and negative themes and characters in curricula, books, and audiovisual materials.
    - Assess for emotional, psychological, and relational difficulties.
    - When in doubt, do something!

For Discussion

- Discuss the strengths and limitations to using the psychological autopsy as a research method.

- The study resulted in a large number of unanswered questions. Select one of these questions and comment on it in relation to gifted individuals.

- Investigate what systems or procedures exist in your school/community to deal with students who exhibit warning signs of potential suicide.

Where We Have Been and Where We Are Going

This section of the book contains only two pieces. In the first chapter, the work of Margaret Mead, anthropologist extraordinaire, provides a foundation for a further look into our "Changing Times." Anthropological studies of cultural change reveal the complexity of our current state. We are all pioneers, the youth among us even more than the adults. As we work to help gifted students find their way, we must learn about the influences unique to our time.

The final chapter, "Top Ten (plus or minus two) List for the 20th Century," was not one of my regular columns. For *Gifted Child Today*'s end of the millennium issue, several professionals in the field of gifted education were asked to overview what they believed were the most important events that occurred over the past century, with an eye on predicting the future of the field. The ideas conveyed represent my way of thinking, which tends to emphasize connections while trying to understand historical patterns. I also tend to believe that sociopolitical forces influence many of the important trends in educational policy and practice.

Changing
Times

Key Concepts

- Stable and transitional factors in cultural definitions
- Margaret Mead's concepts of postfigurative, cofigurative, and prefigurative culture
- Disintermediation

In a previous chapter, "Gifted Students' Social and Emotional Development in the 21st Century," I attempted to illustrate some of the salient ways in which the lives of gifted students today are significantly different from previous generations. Later in that chapter, I made a plea to adults to understand that growing up in a time not experienced by previous generations requires us to act in ways that are not necessarily the ways we think we should. In this chapter, I continue the theme by drawing on the works of the very famous anthropologist Margaret Mead, as well as from some less well-known contemporary authors.

As a researcher interested in how we can guide gifted children's development in the psychological realm to help them become as healthy, happy, and successful as possible, I often read other scholars' accounts of where we are as a nation and world, where we have been, and where we are going. From my readings, I try to select the meaningful from the less meaningful. I have come to believe in a few of what I consider relatively stable factors, some variables that are in transition, and some important variables that are changing rapidly in important ways.

The first rather stable factor is that the United States is made up of a large number of cities, towns, and hamlets, with untold numbers of ghettos, communities, and villages. Across this array of living conditions are the myriad other ways people vary (e.g., ethnically, racially, religiously, regionally). Hence, when we think of the lives of our gifted students, we have to acknowledge that there is no one United States per se, but instead we have hundreds of differing influences factoring into the specifics of the lived experience of being gifted as an American. The specifics of the experience can be put under a loose interpretation of the notion of the culture in which a person lives.

An example of an important convention cutting across the enormous variation in the United States that has significant impact on gifted children's lives (perhaps not equally, however) is the institution of marriage. At the same time as the change in the divorce rate in the U.S., there has also appeared a change in the manifestations of the nuclear family that includes increasing numbers of hybrid families and single-parent homes. There are some obvious and some less-obvious outcomes of these types of changes on the psychological well-being of gifted students.

The next important factor is an example of one in transition. I include Mead's description of how our society has been evolving over the past generations. In 1970, Margaret Mead described a new cultural trend born of the technological changes of the past century. She noted that early cultures were easily transmitted from generation to generation because individuals always lived close to home. Three generations—children, parents, and grandparents—existed together in the same place. She called this a *postfigurative* culture, and in it a child's life would be predictably like his or her grandparents'. As travel increased and young people moved away from their families, children's lives no longer mirrored their grandparents' lives, so the young people looked to their peers or other adults for cultural definition. Therefore, according to Mead, in this *cofigurative* culture, young people rely on the experience of their elders to a point; but, after that, they must learn from the members of their new place how to fit in. Mead claims that advances in technology have made Americans immigrants both in place, as we have become a transient society, and in time, as our world has changed so rapidly through technology. Hence, our new *prefigurative* culture must create its own society without a dependence on the experiences of our elders. Mead (1970) described an erroneous assumption adults often hold about their and subsequent generations:

> It is assumed by the adult generation that there still is general agreement about the good, the true, and the beautiful and that human nature, complete with built-in ways of perceiving, thinking, feeling, and acting, is essentially constant. Such beliefs are, of course, wholly incompatible with a full appreciation of the findings of anthropology, which has documented the fact that innovations in technology and in the form of institutions inevitably bring about alterations in cultural character. It is astonishing to see how readily a belief in change can be integrated with a belief in changelessness, even in cultures whose members have access to voluminous historical records and who agree that history consists not merely of currently desirable constructs but of verifiable facts. (p. 60)

The third category of factors that are important and changing very rapidly continues from Mead's quote. The growth of the personal computer, generally, and the emergence of the Internet, specifically, are illustrating an important example of what Mead claimed more than 30 years ago: "innovations in technology and in the form of institutions inevitably bring about alterations in cultural character" (p. 60). An early example of this type of effect can be found in the South. Numerous books have been written about Southern hospitality, particularly as it pertains to impromptu social interactions on sidewalks, porches, streets, and the like. Where people crossed paths, a gracious interaction took place. With the new technology of air conditioning came many fewer outdoor interactions of both strangers and friends alike. The effect of two generations having grown up with air conditioning has changed some of the cultural expectations for what it is to be Southern. Over time, these cultural expectations will be lost, to a large extent because of the effects of technology.

A more contemporary example of technology affecting our culture is still relatively early in its development. It is the overall effect of relying on computers for several types of activities that have typically required social interactions among various groups of people. Arguably, the most developed of these types of activities is the purchasing of products or services using the Internet. The most noticeable aspect of the development of the Internet over the past 5 years has been its commercialization. Monumental efforts to make available all types of products for purchase have seemingly driven the development of the Internet. Everything from automobiles to opportunities to gamble can be purchased while sitting in one's home. These are ingredients for cultural change: opportunity, control, anonymity, and convenience. In a recent lecture, software engineer and author Ellen Ullman (2000) described the marketing term *disintermediation* as a goal for businesses intent on using the Internet to separate the purchaser from everything except what is being bought. Disintermediation establishes the single consumer sitting at home, often alone, as the most powerful force in purchasing. To accomplish this goal, advertisers have marketed such concepts as this one found on the billboard of the San Francisco theater: "Now the world really does revolve around you." Ullman went on to claim that the effects of this technology and marketing over time promotes the "my" mentality in a very powerful way: "the 'My Computer' icon bothers me on the Windows desktop, baby names like 'My Yahoo' and 'My Snap'; my, my, my; 2-year-old talk; infantilizing and condescending" (p. 31). Advertising slogans such as "Wouldn't you rather be at home?" along with the rapid advancements in technology have been projected to lead to a total individuation of experiences. For example, Ullman cited a museum owner's comments that soon extensive art holdings accessible through the Internet will lead to people establishing exhibits only representing their personal interests. His example, "Today I visited the museum of me. I liked it," is indicative of the wave about to affect our society.

Innumerable outcomes will potentially come from this shifting to the individual as the most valued. Two are the idea that civil space will no longer be needed and that the only place of pleasure and satisfaction is your home. As adults needing to guide gifted children, we must appreciate the substantial diversity making up the United States, understand the changes in the family structures in ways that honor the natural diversity that comes from cultural evolution, and learn what we can in the general arena of technology. From this wisdom we should be able to accommodate the ever-changing social and emotional needs of all children, including gifted children.

For Discussion

- Discuss how changes in family structures may impact the psychological well-being of gifted students.

- Margaret Mead noted that "It is astonishing to see how readily a belief in change can be integrated with a belief in change-lessness." Comment on this in relation to giftedness and school systems.

- Provide further examples of how technology has influenced cultural traditions or expectations.

Top Ten (plus or minus two) List for the 20th Century

Key Concepts

- Psychometrically based pedagogy
- Influence of Binet, Terman, Freud, Watson, Thorndike, Skinner, Gardner, and Sternberg on gifted education
- Influence of Sputnik launch, civil rights laws, Public Law 94-142, learning theory, brain-based research, Jacob Javits legislation, the National Research Center on the Gifted and Talented, changing U.S. demographics on gifted education

---

The following represents ideas about some of the most influential events, circumstances, or decisions to affect gifted education over the past 100 years. Some of the events are well known, while others may not be known at all. Some of the circumstances reflect the world according to Tracy, while others are quite possibly part of history that has been, or one day will be written about. Some of the decisions represent my take on them and may be arguable as facts, while others may represent a consensus in the field. In short, the ideas expressed here may not represent the folks at *Gifted Child Today*, Prufrock Press, or any other living, breathing person. They have been fun to think about, and the process has helped me clarify some of the underpinnings on which I base other ideas. While I doubt that this list will become a historical road map for the field of gifted education, I hope it becomes the impetus for others to ponder this subject.

One of the assumptions I operated under while working on my list was that, because I knew that a couple of very capable thinkers were working on the same assignment, there would probably be some overlap in our lists. Consequently, I used that assumption to take some liberties with the charge. In a final prefacing comment, I would like to note that, once given this assignment by Dr. Susan Johnsen, I started generating items for top ten lists. I worked on this by carrying around a pad and pencil for a couple of months. To date, I have created 14 different top ten lists. I even lost one. A few of the lists were created as I woke up in the middle of the night having had what I thought at the time was an epiphany. Several of those lists were ripped to shreds, burned, then buried. So much for the creativity of my unconscious mind. This list is really an amalgam of ideas that seemed to reappear across the numerous lists generated, or seemed to reflect ideas that might not get me drummed out of the field if I actually wrote them down. To make my thinking understandable in an efficient manner, I will tie together ideas that I believe are indicators and/or examples of the point I am trying to make. By explaining them, they may appear to be discrete from each other. In many cases, however, the ideas are connected, and in some cases, one idea sets the stage for the next, not necessarily in a planned way, but more like the ways in which ideas are shown to lead to others on the PBS series *Connections*. One final wringing of hands: My way of thinking is highly contextually driven. Consequently, the ideas will not be as detailed as I tend to imagine them.

Rather than count down from ten to one, I will offer a set of ten (or so), starting with events in the late 1800s. I will call this set of events "From the Apgar Score to the Licensing Exam," or "The Reign of Standardized Testing." Better yet, number 10 is the emergence of efficient ways for making important educational decisions. Let me use the phrase *psychometrically based pedagogy*. I will credit the development of the Binet intelligence test as the earliest influence. From Binet came the Army Alpha and Beta tests, the Stanford Binet, Wechsler series and a host of other efforts to measure a person's intellectual ability (and everything else about them, as well). The efficiency of group intelligence tests allowed decisions to be made in a highly time-efficient manner that, in my mind, set the standard for high-stakes testing. For example, doing poorly on the Army tests increased one's chances of going to the front during World War I as a foot soldier, where they died at a higher rate than those in other positions. The attitude was created, or at least reflected, in these practices that psychometric principles should be the basis for making hard decisions about young people's roles and responsibilities in the United States. From this period emerged the original Terman (1925) studies on intelligence. His work reflected the science and views of people of the era, yielding arguably the single most important study underpinning the field of gifted education today. While it is unfair and anachronistic to hold Terman's research to all the considerations and criteria of research conducted today, it is a fair statement that some in the field of gifted education have determined that the Terman research is quite limited in its representation of the many conceptions of giftedness that are popular today. Even with these concerns, I believe that the influence of the Terman research on today's ideas of giftedness cannot be overestimated. The research also added support for the use of standardized intelligence tests and to the conception of giftedness described in the studies. Moreover, the term IQ has become so ingrained in the American vernacular and psyche, that groups of adults belong to clubs based on their IQ test score. The last name of Albert Einstein has become synonymous with a high IQ score. "He's no Einstein" is a criticism often used to describe people thought to be dull.

During this time in history, Sigmund Freud was quite prominent in influencing beliefs about the nature of people. While his views are both interesting and insightful, they did little to help the relatively young public school system accommodate the increasing numbers of immigrant children needing, expecting, and being forced to participate in schooling. Fortunately for the schools, John Watson and Edward Thorndike were setting the stage for Fred (a.k.a. B. F.) Skinner to provide some of the underpinnings needed to educate vast numbers of children from modest means. Skinner, Thorndike, and other behaviorists reified the concepts of a type of psychology and became the architects of mass schooling. While Terman's influence helped establish an entity notion of giftedness—that giftedness is a thing that can be measured—the behaviorists influenced later writers to think that looking at the behaviors of children is a more important concern than relying on paper- and pencil-tests. The behaviorist view of teaching and learning required teachers to teach from the smallest concept to the larger idea by chaining. More importantly, however, behaviorists' mechanistic views of humankind challenged our basic core beliefs about people. Behaviors are learned; therefore, giftedness can be influenced. With these ideas, the early seeds were sown to add environmental influences to our prevailing concept of genius. Clearly, despite the fact that early philosophers had already espoused both positions, their influence was not so great as the philosopher psychologists in the first half of the 20th century.

In 1957, the Russians launched Sputnik. From all accounts, this event led the United States to begin an aggressive effort to catch up with the Russians in the space race. Of course, the Cold War and the fear that the Russians would dominate the world fueled this race. From this single event, numerous national, state, and local efforts to better prepare students in math and science were begun. For several years, educating students in mathematical and scientific areas seemed to be a high priority for the U.S. Prior to this period and for many years following, Albert Einstein was one of the most recognized and respected people in the world. His popularity was that of a celebrity—the Michael Jordan of the era. Children aspired to be like Einstein.

In the 1960s, a cultural and civil rights revolution was in full force. From fashion, to political attitudes, to one's very personal aspirations, ideals were changing. Dr. Martin Luther King Jr., Rosa Parks, and many others sought to bring to all people the same opportunities as those enjoyed by the people who had maintained power since the early years of the country. The Civil Rights Law, passed in 1964, signaled what I believe to be one of the three most important influences on gifted education. While it is hard to imagine, prior to 1964, and, to some extent, today, children of color have been left out of educational efforts to maximize talent.

The next event that has had a significant impact on gifted education was the passage of Public Law 94–142 in 1974. This law effectively required schools to provide appropriate educational services to students with disabilities. When one reviews the history of public schools in the United States, few single events have had more impact on the overall practices of schools throughout the U.S. than this law. While I am somewhat disappointed that gifted students did not become a direct part of this law as a protected group, I believe that the law's influence on the American understanding of education and the responsibility we have to accommodate the needs of exceptional students did have a tremendous impact on the lives of gifted students.

Between 1974 and today, one topic (conceptions of intelligence) has been widely written about both in the popular press and scholarly journals. The articles have had a tremendous impact on educators' thinking and, to a large extent, have pushed along our notions of gift-edness. While many of the contemporary notions of giftedness are not limited to an intelligence-based foundation, the field of gifted education is both underpinned by it and somewhat held hostage to populists' notions of intelligence. In 1983, the book *Frames of Mind* by Howard Gardner was published. Soon thereafter, another view of intelligence by Robert Sternberg was published. Since the mid-1980s, numerous views have emerged. This public debate has been broad, with public school educators leading the way. It was clear that our traditional IQ-based notion of intelligence was too narrow to reflect the experiences of our nation's educators. Nothing was more powerful than an idea whose time had come. In essence, teachers were rejecting many psychologists' ideas about intelligence.

In a parallel theme that is more pervasive and yet more subtle, public school teachers have been wrestling away from psychologists the mantle of defining what learning is and how it is done. Teachers had grown quite disillusioned with the touted research of famous psychologists about what should work with students in classrooms. After many years of being criticized for not teaching in ways that reflect the researchers' ideas of teaching and learning, public school teachers have joined with philosophers and a different group of psychologists in claiming that students construct their understanding. This constructivist view of the world is popular among teachers and professors of education. Many learning theorists in psychology still maintain rather traditional views of how students learn. Those in society who determine the views of intelligence and learning theory that are institutionally supported are the most influential political groups in all of public education. For many years, the IQ-based definition dominated the scene and was widely accepted by the general populace. However, since 1983, the de facto control over the application of definitions of intelligence (giftedness) and learning theory has ostensibly shifted from academics in universities to professional educators in public schools.

It will be fascinating over the next 20 years to monitor the most recent popular topic of research drawing considerable attention from researchers, professional educators, and lay people alike: brain-based research. While I am personally optimistic that important findings will be yielded from this line of research, we will undoubtedly have to live through periods of time when pedestrian notions of the research will affect classroom practices. For example, brain hemisphericity was the topic of many articles in the popular press some years ago, as were books on teaching to a child's right brain or left brain. This "movement" was so influential that teachers would describe children as "right-brained" or "left-brained."

The next major event reflects the evolution of pedagogy, changing from a rather inflexible practice of grade skipping to the various options that have been created over the past 40 years or so. Gifted education was not very appealing to parents and teachers when they worried that the only option for little Janie was for her to skip a grade or two. Today, teachers have myriad options that include grade skipping, teaching techniques that attempt to differentiate the curriculum, and state-funded residential schools. Other options include Saturday and summer programs such as Governor's Schools, and the various talent search programs. While the impetus behind these examples is quite different, I believe that the second set of options (differentiation) will continue to attract supporters among school personnel. The attraction is the result of two things: (a) teachers are the primary decision makers when curricular differentiation is being implemented, and (b) it fits the inclusive model of education toward which many public schools are moving. Two important undercurrents to the support of an inclusion model of instruction are that it has a face validity of egalitarianism and that the term *gifted* is not used. Other historical events have accelerated the acceptance of differentiation. For example, after some early problems with the notion of gifted education, the middle school movement has warmed up to differentiation due to the relentless work of professionals like Carol Tomlinson who have presented at numerous conferences and written books that translate the tenets of differentiation into attractive language for general educators and administrators. Another factor important to this equation is the inclusion movement. Curricular differentiation makes great sense in heterogeneous classrooms.

Another recent event that has had an impact on gifted education has come from the confluence of several situations. The funding of Jacob Javits legislation and the subsequent birth of the National Research Center on the Gifted and Talented have brought increased attention to the needs of gifted students. Increased research and publications have also been an important by-product of these events. At the same time, the National Association for Gifted Children and the Council for Exceptional Children's Division—The Association for the Gifted have joined together to influence politicians about the nature and needs of gifted students. These two groups have also worked in collaboration with numerous other important professional educational groups to influence the national educational agenda relative to gifted education.

I believe that the changing demographic make-up of people in the United States has had an important impact on the thinking in gifted education over the past 20 years or so. I also believe that the influence will eventually have the greatest impact of any single event or circumstance. As the dominant group in our society that has been serviced directly by gifted education (Caucasian, middle-class males) grows ever smaller in the demographic equation, the more power other groups will have. Although the field of gifted education is still quite inadequate in applying some of the contemporary conceptions of giftedness, the issues surrounding them are being discussed, intellectual restlessness is present, and conflicting ideas are omnipresent. In essence, the stage has been set for many of the nontraditional ideas for defining giftedness, identifying gifted children, and providing services for them to be tested and researched. It will be interesting to see if another type of civil rights movement emerges that is driven by the notion of maximizing the school-related talent of all gifted children. If this type of movement gains momentum, I doubt that the way to resolve the historic disparities among groups of gifted children will be based on psychometric tweaking of instruments. Implicit in these comments is the argument from the critical theory perspective that benefits made available to a society's children reflect the current power structure. Enhancing the opportunities for underrepresented gifted children will require a type of revolution. Whether the field of gifted education has the ability or will to change practices to the extent that it creates the same degree of potential for maximizing all gifted children's abilities is doubtful. However, many bright, dedicated people from various backgrounds are working hard to bring about those opportunities. Changing the basic structure of our schooling practices is a difficult thing to accomplish. Of course, the proving ground for many of these experiments may very well be in regular classroom settings.

I have chosen to end this chapter by cataloging some of the other trends and issues that I expect to have an effect on the direction and progress of the field of gifted education over the next 50 years. Other mediating trends may include: our confused notions of what giftedness is; the nation's economy; site-based management; individual school boards; national legislation; the evolution of computers and their effect on the practices of schooling; the politicization of schooling; and the goals of schooling. I think the goals we hold for our schools are largely met. I believe that, if we truly expected our schools to maximize the potential of all gifted students by educating learned people who can function well in a democracy, many aspects of our schools would change. Because our society holds confused views about gifted students, gifted students necessarily receive mixed messages every day of their lives. The people who hold these confused views include all walks of life, from architects, to physicians, to teachers, to teacher trainers, and even to the gifted students themselves. I believe that, until a coherent message about giftedness can be crafted that opens doors for the greatest number of gifted children rather than letting only a very small number through, then society will remain discontented with schooling. Some prescribe a panacea of school choice as a remedy for their criticisms of our public schools. The criticisms are representative of one aspect of the problems with which schools struggle in trying to educate gifted students. That is, under this prescription, children are treated as commodities, as capital for our nation's economy. There is benefit to students becoming employable, but wouldn't it be nice if our goal was to educate people to be the best people they can be?

For Discussion

- What do you believe are the most important events influencing pedagogical practices that have occurred over the past century?

References

Allen, R. E. (Ed.). (1996). *The Reader's Digest Oxford complete wordfinder*. Pleasantville, NY: Reader's Digest Association.

Bronfenbrenner, U. (1994). Ecological models of human development. In T. Husen & T. N. Postlethwaite (Eds.), *International encyclopedia of education* (2nd ed., Vol. 3, pp. 1643–1647). Oxford: Pergamon Press/Elsevier Science.

Buescher, T. (1985). A framework for understanding the social and emotional development of gifted and talented students. *Roeper Review, 8,* 10–15.

Capuzzi, D., & Golden, L. (Eds.). (1988). *Preventing adolescent suicide.* Muncie, IN: Accelerated Development.

Coleman, L. J. (1985). *Schooling the gifted.* New York: Addison Wesley.

Coleman, L. J., & Cross, T. L. (1988). Is being gifted a social handicap? *Journal for the Education of the Gifted, 11,* 41–56.

Coleman, L. J., & Cross, T. L. (2001). *Being gifted in school: An introduction to development, guidance, and teaching.* Waco, TX: Prufrock Press.

Costello, R. B. (Ed.). (1992). *Webster's college dictionary.* New York: Random House.

Cross, T. L. (2001). Gifted children and Erikson's theory of psychosocial development. *Gifted Child Today, 24*(1), 54–55.

Cross, T. L. (in press). Guiding the psychosocial development of gifted students in a residential setting. In *Talent Development: Vol. 4. The Fifth Biennial Henry B. & Jocelyn Wallace National Research Symposium on Talent Development.*

Cross, T. L., Coleman, L. J., & Terhaar-Yonkers, M. (1991). The social cognition of gifted adolescents in schools: Managing the stigma of giftedness. *Journal for the Education of the Gifted, 15,* 44–55.

Cross, T., Cook, R., & Dixon, D. (1996). Psychological autopsies of three academically talented adolescents who committed suicide. *Journal of Secondary Gifted Education, 7,* 403–409.

Davidson, L., & Linnoila, M. (1991). *Risk factors for youth suicide.* Washington, DC: National Institute of Mental Health.

Delisle, J. (1986). Death with honors: Suicide and the gifted adolescent. *Journal of Counseling and Development, 64,* 558–560.

Dweck, C. S. (1986). Motivation processes affecting learning. *American Psychologist, 41,* 1040–1048.

Ebert, B. (1987). Guide to conducting a psychological autopsy. *Professional Psychology: Research and Practice, 18,* 52–56.

Erikson, E. H. (1963). *Childhood and society* (2nd ed.). New York: Norton.

Erikson, E. H. (1972). Autobiographical notes on the identity crisis. In G. Holton (Ed.), *The twentieth-century sciences: Studies in the biography of ideas.* New York: Norton.

Gardner, H. (1983). *Frames of mind: The theory of multiple intelligences.* New York: BasicBooks.

Hall, G. S. (1904). *Adolescence: Its psychology and its relations to physiology, anthropology, sociology, sex, crime, religion, and education.* New York: Appleton.

Holinger, P. C., Offer, D., Barter, J. T., & Bell, C. C. (1994). *Suicide and homicide among adolescents.* New York: Guilford Press.

Jones, D. (1977). Suicide by aircraft: A case report. *Aviation, Space, and Environmental Medicine, 48,* 454–459.

Kaiser, C. F., & Berndt, D. J. (1985). Predictors of loneliness in the gifted adolescent. *Gifted Child Quarterly, 29,* 74–77.

Katz, J. (2001). *Voices from the hellmouth.* Retrieved September 21, 2003, from http://slashdot.org/articles/99/04/25/1438249.shtml

Kozol, J. (1991). *Savage inequalities: Children in America's schools.* New York: Crown.

Ludwig, A. L. (1995). *The price of greatness: Resolving the creativity and madness controversy.* New York: Guilford.

May, R. (1969). The emergence of existential psychology. In R. May (Ed.), *Existential psychology* (pp. 1–48). New York: Random House.

Mead, M. (1970). *Culture and commitment.* Garden City, NY: Natural History Press.

Neill, K., Benensohn, H., Farber, A., & Resnick, H. (1974). The psychological autopsy: A technique for investigating a hospital suicide. *Hospital and Community Psychiatry, 25,* 33–36.

Offer, D., & Offer, J. B. (1975). *From teenage to young manhood.* New York: BasicBooks.

Piechowski, M. (1979). Developmental potential. In N. Colangelo & T. Zaffron (Eds.), *New voices in counseling the gifted* (pp. 25–57). Dubuque, IA: Kendall/Hunt.

Terman, L. M. (1925). *Genetic studies of genius: Vol. 1. Mental and physical traits of a thousand gifted children.* Stanford, CA: Stanford University Press.

Tomlinson-Keasey, C., & Keasey, B. (1988). "Signatures" of suicide. In D. Capuzzi & Golden (Eds.), *Preventing adolescent suicide* (pp. 213–245). Muncie, IN: Accelerated Development.

Ullman, E. (2000, May). Wouldn't you rather be at home? The Internet and the myth of the powerful self. *Harper's*, 30–33.

Resources

Gifted Education Journals and Publications

Gifted Child Quarterly
Paula Olszewski-Kubilius, Editor
Center for Talent Development
Northwestern University
617 Dartmouth Pl.
Evanston, IL 60208-4175
Phone: (847) 491-3782
Fax: (847) 467-4283
E-mail: pkubilus@casbah.acns.nwu.edu
Web site: http://www.nagc.org/Publications/GiftedChild

Gifted Child Today
Susan Johnsen, Editor
Baylor University
P.O. Box 87304
Waco, TX 76798-7304
Phone: (254) 710-6116
E-mail: Susan_Johnsen@baylor.edu
Web site: http://www.prufrock.com/prufrock_jm_giftchild.cfm

Gifted Education Communicator
Margaret Gosfield, Editor
Gifted Education Communicator
15141 E. Whittier Blvd., Ste. 510
Whittier, CA 90603
Phone: (562) 789-9933
E-mail: CAGoffice@aol.com
Web site: http://CAGifted.org

Gifted and Talented International
JoyceVanTassel-Baska, Editor
College of William and Mary
P.O. Box 8795
Williamsburg, VA 23187-8795
Phone: (757) 221-2185
Fax: (757) 221-2184
E-mail: jlvant@facstaff.wm.edu
Web site: http://www.worldgifted.org/xpubs.htm

Journal for the Education of the Gifted
Laurence J. Coleman, Editor
Dept. of Early Childhood, Special Education, & Physical Education
University of Toledo
Mail Stop #106
2801 West Bancroft
Toledo, OH 43606-2290
Phone: (419) 530-2626
E-mail: laurence.coleman@utoledo.edu
Web site: http://www.prufrock.com/prufrock_jm_jeg.cfm

Journal of Secondary Gifted Education
Bonnie Cramond, Editor
Department of Educational Psychology
University of Georgia
323 Aderhold Hall
Athens, GA 30602-7143
Phone: (706) 542-4248
Web site: http://www.prufrock.com/mag_jsge.html

Parenting for High Potential
Don Treffinger, Editor
Center for Creative Learning
P.O. Box 14100, NE Plaza
Sarasota, FL 34278-4100
Phone: (941) 342-9928
Fax: (941) 342-0064
E-mail: ideadoc@comcast.net; cclofc@gte.net
Web site: http://www.nagc.org/Publications/Parenting/#top

Roeper Review
Tracy L. Cross, Editor
Indiana Academy, Ball State University
Muncie, IN 47306
Phone: (765) 285-7457
Fax: (765) 285-2777
E-mail: tcross@bsu.edu; info@roeperreview.org
Web site: http://www.roeperreview.org

Understanding Our Gifted
Dorothy Knopper, Publisher
Open Space Communications
P.O. Box 18268
Boulder, CO 80308
Phone: (303) 444-7020
Fax: (303) 545-6505
E-mail: Dorothy@openspacecomm.com
Web site: http://www.openspacecomm.com

United States
National Gifted Associations

American Association for Gifted Children (AAGC)
Duke University
P.O. Box 90270
Durham, NC 27708-0270
Margaret Evans Gayle, Executive Director
Phone: (919) 783-6152
Web site: http://www.aagc.org

Council for Exceptional Children (CEC)
1110 N. Glebe Rd., Suite 300
Arlington, VA 22201-5704
Phone: (888) 232-7733; (703) 620-3660
TTY: (866) 915-5000
Fax: (703) 264-9494
E-mail: service@cec.sped.org
Web site: http://www.cec.sped.org

The Association for the Gifted (TAG)
Gloria Taradash
Initiatives for Education
26 Cedar Hill Pl. NE
Albuquerque, NM 87122
Phone/Fax: (505) 828-1001
E-mail: gtaradash@aol.com
Web site: http://www.cectag.org

National Association of Gifted Children (NAGC)
1701 L St. NW Ste. 550
Washington, DC 20036
Phone: (202) 785-4268
Web site: http://www.nagc.org

The National Foundation for Gifted and Creative Children (NFGCC)
395 Diamond Hill Road
Warwick, RI 02886-8554
Phone: (401) 738-0937
Web site: http://www.nfgcc.org/

Supporting the Emotional Needs of the Gifted (SENG)
P.O. Box 6550
Scottsdale, AZ 85261
Phone: (773) 528-2113
E-mail: sengifted@sbcglobal.net
Web site: http://www.sengifted.org/default.htm

Centers for Gifted Education

Center for Creative Learning
Don Treffinger, President
P.O. Box 14100, NE Plaza
Sarasota, FL 34278-4100
Phone: (941) 342-9928; Fax: (941) 342-0064
E-mail: cclofc@gte.net
Web site: http://www.creativelearning.com

The Center for Gifted
Joan Franklin Smutny, Director
National-Louis University
P.O. Box 364
Wilmette, IL 60091
Phone: (847) 256-5150
E-mail: jrinne@nl.edu
Web site: http://www.centerforgifted.com

Center for Gifted Education
Ann Robinson
University of Arkansas at Little Rock
Gifted Programs
2801 S. University Ave.
Little Rock, AR 72204
E-mail: aerobinson@ualr.edu
Web site: http://www.ualr.edu/~giftedpro

Center for Gifted Education
Jeanette P. Parker, Director
University of Louisiana–Lafayette
P.O. Box 44872
Lafayette, LA 70504-4872
Phone: (337) 482-6701
Fax: (337) 482-5842
E-mail: parker@louisiana.edu
Web site: http://www.coe.louisiana.edu/centers/gifted.html

Center for Gifted Education
Margo Long, Director
Whitworth College
300 W. Hawthorne Road
Spokane, WA 99251
Phone: (509) 777-3226
E-mail: gifted@whitworth.edu.
Web site: http://www.whitworth.edu/Academic/Department/
Education/Gifted/Index.htm

The Center for Gifted Education
Joyce VanTassel-Baska, Executive Director
College of William and Mary
P.O. Box 8795
Williamsburg, VA 23187-8795
Phone: (757) 221-2362
Fax: (757) 221-2184
Web site: http://www.cfge.wm.edu

The Center for Gifted Studies
Julia Roberts, Director
Western Kentucky University
1 Big Red Way
Bowling Green, KY 42101-3576
Phone: (270) 745-6323
Fax: (270) 745-6279
E-mail: gifted@wku.edu
Web site: http://www.wku.edu/gifted

Center for Gifted Studies and Talent Development
Cheryll M. Adams, Director
Ball State University
Muncie, IN 47306
Phone: (765) 285-5390
E-mail: cadams@bsu.edu
Web site: http://www.bsu.edu/teachers/services/ctr

Center for Talent Development
Paula Olszewski-Kubilius, Director
School of Education and Social Policy
Northwestern University
617 Dartmouth Pl.
Evanston, IL 60208-4175
Phone: (847) 491-3782
Fax: (847) 467-4283
E-mail: ctd@nwu.edu
Web site: http://www.ctd.northwestern.edu

Center for Talented Youth (CTY)
Lea Ybarra, Executive Director
Johns Hopkins University
3400 N. Charles St.
Baltimore, MD 21218
Phone: (410) 516-0337
Fax: (410) 516-0804
E-mail: ctyinfo@jhu.edu
Web site: http://www.jhu.edu/gifted

Centre for Gifted Education
University of Calgary
170 Education Block
2500 University Dr. NW
Calgary, Alberta, Canada T2N 1N4
Phone: (403) 220-7799
Fax: (403) 210-2068
E-mail: gifteduc@ucalgary.ca
Web site: http://www.ucalgary.ca/~gifteduc

DISCOVER Projects
C. June Maker
Department of Special Education
Rehabilitation & School Psychology
College of Education
University of Arizona
Tucson, AZ 85721-0069
Phone: (520) 622-8106
Fax: (520) 621-3821
E-mail: discover@email.arizona.edu
Web site: http://discover.arizona.edu

Drury College Center for Gifted Education
Drury College
900 N. Benton Ave.
Springfield, MO 65802
Phone: (800) 922-2274
Web site: http://www.drury.edu/multinl/story.cfm?
ID=1620&NLID=150

Duke University Talent Identification Program (TIP)
P.O. Box 90747
Durham, NC 27708
Phone: (919) 684-3847
Fax: (919) 681-7921
E-mail: information@tip.duke.edu
Web site: http://www.tip.duke.edu/

The Frances A. Karnes Center for Gifted Studies
Frances A. Karnes, Director
University of Southern Mississippi
P.O. Box 8207
Hattiesburg, MS 39406-8207
Phone: (601) 266-5236
Fax: (601) 266-4978
E-mail: Gifted.Studies@usm.edu
Web site: http://www-dept.usm.edu/~gifted

Gifted Development Center
Linda Kreger Silverman
1452 Marion St.
Denver, CO 80218
Phone: (303) 837-8378
Fax: (303) 831-7465
E-mail: gifted@gifteddevelopment.com
Web site: http://www.gifteddevelopment.com

Gifted Education Resource Institute (GERI)
Sidney M. Moon, Director
Purdue University
Beering Hall, Rm. 5113
100 N. University St.
West Lafayette, IN 47907-2098
Phone: (765) 494-7243
Fax: (765) 496-2706
E-mail: geri@soe.purdue.edu
Web site: http://www.geri.soe.purdue.edu

Leta Hollingworth Center for the Study and Education of the Gifted
James Borland and Lisa R. Wright, Directors
Teachers College, Columbia University
TC Box 170
309 E. Main St.
New York, NY 10027
Phone: (212) 678-3871
E-mail: borland@exchange.tc.columbia.edu
E-mail: LWright@exchange.tc.columbia.edu
Web site: http://www.tc.columbia.edu/centers/hollingworth

National Research Center on the Gifted and Talented (NRC/GT)
Carolyn Callahan, Director
University of Virginia
Curry School of Education
P.O. Box 400277
Charlottesville, VA 22904-4277
Phone: (804) 924-4557
Fax: (804) 982-2383
E-mail: NRCGT@virginia.edu
Web site: http://curry.edschool.virginia.edu/go/NRC

Naeg Center for Gifted Education and Talent Development
University of Connecticut
2131 Hillside Road, Unit 3007
Storrs, CT 06269-3007
Phone: (860) 486-4826
Fax: (860) 486-2900
Web site: http://www.gifted.uconn.edu

Torrance Center for Creativity and Talent Development
Department of Educational Psychology
323 Aderhold Hall
University of Georgia
Athens, GA 30602-7146
Phone: (706) 542-5104
Fax: (706) 542-4659
E-mail: creative@uga.edu
Web site: http://www.coe.uga.edu/torrance

State Gifted Associations
and Departments of Education

U.S. Department of Education
400 Maryland Ave. SW
Washington, DC 20202-0498
Phone: (800) 872-5327
Web site: http://www.ed.gov/index.jsp

Alabama

Alabama Association for Gifted Children (AAGC)
c/o Hibbett Middle School (membership address)
1601 Appleby Blvd.
Florence, AL 35630
Kay Simpson (AAGC President-elect)
Phone: (256) 768-2800
E-mail: kgsimpson@fcs.k12.al.us
Web site: http://www.aagc.freeservers.com/aagc.html

Alabama Department of Education
50 N. Ripley St.
P.O. Box 302101
Montgomery, AL 36104
Phone: (334) 242-9700
Web site: http://www.alsde.edu/html/home.asp

Alaska

Alaska Department of Education and Early Development
801 W. 10th St., Ste. 200
Juneau, AK 99801-1878
Phone: (907) 465-2800
Fax: (907) 465-3452
Web site: http://www.eed.state.ak.us
Special Education Web site: http://www.educ.state.ak.us/TLS/
sped/home.html

Arizona

Arizona Association for Gifted and Talented
P.O. Box 31088
Phoenix, AZ 85046-1088
Web site: http://www.azagt.org

Arizona Department of Education
1535 W. Jefferson St.
Phoenix, AZ 85007
Phone: (602) 542-4361
Web site: http://www.ade.state.az.us/

Office of Gifted Education
Exceptional Student Services
Peter Laing
Phone: (602) 364-4017
Fax: (602) 542-5404
E-mail: plaing@ade.az.gov
Web site: http://www.ade.state.az.us/ess/gifted

Arkansas

Arkansas Department of Education
#4 Capital Mall
Little Rock, AR 72201
Phone: (501) 682-4475
Web site: http://arkedu.state.ar.us/index.htm

Gifted and Talented Education
Ann Biggers, Administrator
Phone: (501) 682-4224
Web site: http://arkedu.state.ar.us/directory/school_improvement.
html#Gifted

California

California Association for the Gifted (CAG)
15141 E. Whittier Blvd., Ste. 510
Whittier, CA 90603
Phone: (562) 789-9933
Fax: (562) 789-9833
E-mail: cagoffice@aol.com
Web site: http://www.cagifted.org

California Department of Education
P.O. Box 944272
Sacramento, CA 94244-2720
1430 N. St.
Sacramento, CA 95814
Phone: (916) 319–0791
Web site: http://www.cde.ca.gov

Gifted and Talented Education (GATE)
Kay Garcia
Phone: (916) 323-5832
E-mail: kgarcia@cde.ca.gov
Web site: http://www.cde.gov/cilbranch/gate

Colorado

Colorado Association for Gifted and Talented
P.O. Box 473414
Aurora, CO 80447-3414
E-mail: info@coloradogifted.org
Web site: http://www.coloradogifted.org

Colorado Department of Education
201 E. Colfax Ave.
Denver, CO 80203-1799
Phone: (303) 866-6600
Fax: (303) 830-0793
Web site: http://www.cde.state.co.us

Gifted and Talented Services
Jacquelin Medina
Phone: (303) 866-6652
E-mail: medina_j@cde.state.co.us
Web site: http://www.cde.state.co.us/index_special.htm

Connecticut

Connecticut Association for the Gifted (CAG)
26 Center St.
Greenwich, CT 06870
Web site: http://www.CTGifted.org

Connecticut State Department of Education
165 Capitol Ave.
P.O. Box 2219
Hartford, CT 06145
Phone: (860) 713-6748
Web site: http://www.state.ct.us/sde

Gifted and Talented
Bureau of Curriculum and Instruction
Jeanne Purcell, Consultant
E-mail: jeanne.purcell@po.state.ct.us
Phone: (860) 713-6745
Web site: http://www.state.ct.us/sde/dtl/curriculum/currgift.htm

Delaware

Delaware Department of Education
John G. Townsend Building
401 Federal St.
P. O. Box 1402
Dover, DE 19903-1402
Phone: (302) 739-4601
Fax: (302) 739-4654
Web site: http://www.doe.state.de.us

District of Columbia

State Education Office
441 4th St., NW, Ste. 350 N.
Washington, DC 20001
Phone: (202) 727-6436
Web site: http://seo.dc.gov/main.shtm

Florida

Florida Association for the Gifted (FLAG) and
Parents for Able Learner Students (PALS)
5101 Lake-in-the-Woods Blvd.
Lakeland, FL 33813
Phone: (863) 647-3003
E-mail: Pals222@earthlink.net
Web site: http://come.to/gifted

Florida Department of Education
Office of the Commissioner
Turlington Bldg., Ste. 1514
325 W. Gaines St.
Tallahassee, FL 32399
Phone: (850) 245-0505
Fax: (850) 245-9667
Web site: http://www.fldoe.org

Georgia

Georgia Association for Gifted Children
1579F Monroe Dr., #321
Atlanta, GA 30324
Phone/Fax: (404) 875-2284
Web site: http://www.gagc.org

Georgia Department of Education
Help Desk
2054 Twin Towers East
Atlanta, GA 30334

Phone: (404) 656-2800
Fax: (404) 651-6867
E-mail: help.desk@doe.k12.ga.us
Web site: http://www.gadoe.org

Hawai'i

Hawai'i Department of Education
P.O. Box 2360
Honolulu, HI 96804
Phone: (808) 586-3230
Fax: (808) 586-3234
Web site: http://doe.k12.hi.us

Early Childhood/Gifted Education
Betsy Moneymaker, Specialist
Student Support Services
637 18th Ave., Bldg C., #204
Honolulu, HI 96816
Phone: (808) 733-4476
Fax: (808) 548-5390

Idaho

Idaho-The Association for Gifted/State Advocates for Gifted Education (ITAG/SAGE)
Web site: http://www.itag-sage.org

Idaho State Department of Education
650 W. State St.
P.O. Box 83720
Boise, IA 83720-0027
Phone: (208) 332-6800
Web site: http://www.sde.state.id.us

Gifted and Talented
Phone: (208) 332-6911
Web site: http://www.sde.state.id.us/GiftedTalented

Illinois

Illinois Association for Gifted Children
800 E. Northwest Hwy, Ste. #610
Palatine, IL 60074
Phone: (847) 963-1892
Fax: (847) 963-1893
Web site: http://www.iagcgifted.org

Illinois State Board of Education
100 N. First St.
Springfield, IL 62777
Phone: (217) 782-4321
TTY: (217) 782-1900
Web site: http://www.isbe.net/Default.htm

Indiana

Indiana Association for the Gifted (IAG)
P.O. Box 641
Carmel, IN 46082
Phone: (317) 705-1660
Web site: http://www.iag-online.org

Indiana Department of Education
Room 229, State House
Indianapolis, IN 46204-2798
Voice mail: (317) 232-6610
Fax: (317) 232-8004
Web site: http://ideanet.doe.state.in.us

Gifted and Talented Education
Web site: http://ideanet.doe.state.in.us/exceptional/gt

Iowa

Iowa Talented and Gifted Association (ITAG)
8345 University Blvd., Ste. F-1
Des Moines, IA 50325-1168

Phone: (515) 225-2323
Fax: (515) 225-6363
E-mail: IowaTAG@aol.com
Web site: http://www.uiowa.edu/~itag

Idaho Department of Education
Grimes State Office Building
Des Moines, IA, 50319
Phone: (515) 281-5294
Fax: (515) 242-5988
Web site: http://www.state.ia.us/educate/index.html

Kansas

Kansas Association for the Gifted, Talented, and Creative
P.O. Box 8078
Shawnee Mission, KS 66208-0078
Web site: http://www.kgtc.org

Kansas Department of Education
120 SE 10th Ave.
Topeka, KS 66612-1182
Phone: (785) 296-3201
Fax: (785) 296-7933
Web site: http://www.ksbe.state.ks.us/Welcome.html

Kentucky

Kentucky Association for Gifted Education (KAGE)
P.O. Box 9610
Bowling Green, KY 42102-9610
Phone: (270) 745-4301
Fax: (270) 745-6279
E-mail: kage@wku.edu
Web site: http://www.wku.edu/kage

Kentucky Department of Education
500 Mero St.
18th Floor Capital Plaza Tower

Frankfort, KY 40601
Phone: (502) 564-4770
TTY: (502) 564-4970
Web site: http://www.kde.state.ky.us

Gifted and Talented Education Services
Carla Garr
Phone: (502) 564-2106
E-mail: cgarr@kde.state.ky.us
Web site: http://www.kde.state.ky.us/oapd/curric/gt/default.asp

Louisiana

Louisiana Department of Education
P.O. Box 94064
Baton Rouge, LA 70804-9064
Web site: http://www.doe.state.la.us/DOE/asps/home.asp

Division of Special Populations
Eileen Kendrick
Phone: (225) 342-6110
Fax: (225) 342-5880
E-mail: EKendrick@mail.doe.state.la.us
Web site: http://www.doe.state.la.us/DOE/asps/home.asp?I=GIFTED

Maine

Maine Department of Education
23 State House Station
Augusta, ME 04333-0023
Web site: http://www.state.me.us/education/homepage.htm

Gifted and Talented
Wendy Monthey
Phone: (207) 624-6831
E-mail: wanda.monthey@maine.gov

Maryland

Gifted and Talented Association of Montgomery County
308 Penwood Road
Silver Spring, MD 20901
Phone: (301) 593-1702
E-mail: jhoven@erols.com
Web site: http://www.mcps.k12.md.us/departments/eii/
GT_Resources.html

Maryland Department of Education
200 W. Baltimore St.
Baltimore, MD 21201
Phone: (410) 767-0100
Web site: http://www.msde.state.md.us

Gifted and Talented Education
Carolyn Cooper, Specialist
Phone: (410) 767-0363

Massachusetts

Massachusetts Association for Gifted Education (MAGE)
P.O. Box 1265
Barnstable, MA 02630-2265
Voice mail: (781) 394-5526
Web site: http://www.MASSGifted.org

Massachusetts Department of Education
350 Main St.
Malden, MA 02148-5023
Voice: (781) 338-3000
TTY: (800) 439-0183
Web site: http://www.doe.mass.edu

Michigan

Michigan Alliance for Gifted Education (MAGE)
5355 Northland Dr. NE, Ste. C188
Grand Rapids, MI 49525
Phone: (616) 364-5535
E-mail: migiftedchild@migiftedchild.org
Web site: http://www.migiftedchild.org

Michigan Department of Education
608 W. Allegan
Lansing, MI 48933
E-mail: mdeweb@Michigan.gov
Web site: http://www.michigan.gov/mde

Gifted and Talented Education
David Mills
Phone: (517) 373-4213
E-mail: MillsD@michigan.gov
Web site: http://www.michigan.gov/mde/0,1607,7-140-5233_5988-22992—,00.html

Minnesota

Minnesota Council for the Gifted and Talented
5701 Normandale Road, Ste. 345
Edina, MN 55424
Phone: (952) 848-4906
Web site: http://www.MCGT.net

Minnesota Department of Children, Families, and Learning
1500 Highway 36 W.
Roseville, MN 55113
Phone: (651) 582-8200
Web site: http://education.state.mn.us/stellent/groups/public/documents/translatedcontent/pub_mde_home.jsp

Minnesota Gifted and Talented Development Center (MGTDC)
Mary Pfeifer

Phone: (651) 582-8700
E-mail: mary.pfeifer@state.mn.us
Web site: http://www.educ.state.mn.us/ci/programs/gifted/index.htm

Mississippi

Mississippi Department of Education
359 N. West St., P.O. Box 771
Jackson, MS 39205
Phone: (601) 359-3513
Web site: http://www.mde.k12.ms.us

Gifted Education
Conrad Castle
Phone: (601) 359-2586
Fax: (601) 359-2040
E-mail: ccastle@mde.k12.ms.us
Web site: http://www.mde.k12.ms.us/ovte/ospd/fhapage/
giftedweb%20changes.html

Missouri

Gifted Association of Missouri (GAM)
P.O. Box 1495
Jefferson City, MO 65102
Web site: http://www.mogam.org

Missouri Department of Elementary and Secondary Education
P.O. Box 480
Jefferson City, MO 65102
Phone: (573) 751-4212
Fax: (573) 751-8613
Web site: http://www.dese.state.mo.us

Gifted Education Programs
Davis Welch, Director
Phone: (573) 751-2453
E-mail: dwelsh@mail.dese.state.mo.us
Web site: http://www.dese.state.mo.us/divimprove/gifted

Montana

Montana Association of Gifted and Talented Education
Kathie Bailey, President
E-mail: KGBailey52@yahoo.com
Web site: http://www.mtagate.org

Montana Office of Public Instruction
P.O. Box 202501
Helena, MT 59620-2501
Phone: (888) 231-9393
Web site: http://www.opi.state.mt.us/index.html

Nebraska

Nebraska Association for the Gifted
1201 Kelland Dr.
Norfolk, NE 68701
Linda Engel
E-mail: lengel@esu8.org
E-mail: NebraskaGifted@aol.com
Web site: http://www.NebraskaGifted.org

Nebraska Department of Education
301 Centennial Mall S.
Lincoln, NE 68509-4987
Phone: (402) 471-2295
Web site: http://www.nde.state.ne.us

High Ability Learning
Mary Duffy
Phone: (402) 471-0737
E-mail: mduffy@nde.state.ne.us

Nevada

Nevada Association for Gifted and Talented (NAGT)
P.O. Box 60143
Las Vegas, NV 89160

Phone: (702) 991-9987 (South)
Phone: (775) 852-5019 (North)
Fax: (775) 852-5021
E-mail: info@nevadagt.org
Web site: http://www.nevadagt.org

Nevada Department of Education

700 E. Fifth St.
Carson City, NV 89701
Phone: (775) 687-9200
Fax: (775) 687-9101
Web site: http://www.nde.state.nv.us

Gifted and Talented

Doris Betts
Phone: (775) 782-7647
Web site: http://www.nde.state.nv.us/admin/org/programs.html#g

New Hampshire

New Hampshire Association for Gifted Education (NHAGE)

P.O. Box 6106
Nashua, NH 03063-6106
Web site: http://207.228.215.62

New Hampshire Department of Education

101 Pleasant St.
Concord, NH 03301-3860
Phone: (603) 271-3494
Fax: (603) 271-1953
Web site: http://www.ed.state.nh.us

Gifted and Talented Education

Robert Wells
Phone: (603) 271-1536

New Jersey

New Jersey Association for Gifted Children (NJAGC)
P.O. Box 667
Mt. Laurel, NJ 08054-0667
Phone: (856) 273-7530
E-mail: njagc@yahoo.com
Web site: http://www.njagc.org

New Jersey Department of Education
P.O. Box 500
Trenton, NJ 08625
Phone: (609) 292-4469
Web site: http://www.state.nj.us/education

New Mexico

New Mexico State Department of Education
300 Don Gaspar
Santa Fe, NM 87501-2786
Phone: (505) 827-5800
Web site: http://www.sde.state.nm.us

New York

Advocacy for Gifted and Talented Education in New York (AGATE)
31 Brookline Road
Ballston Spa, NY 12020
Web site: http://www.agateny.org

New York State Education Department
Education Building
Albany, NY 12234
Phone: (518) 474-3852
Web site: http://www.nysed.gov

North Carolina

North Carolina Association for the Gifted and Talented (NCAGT)
Wesley Guthrie
P.O. Box 899
Swansboro, NC 28584-0899
Phone: (910) 326-8463
Fax: (910) 326-8465
Web site: http://www.ncagt.org

North Carolina State Board of Education
6302 Mail Service Center
Raleigh, NC 27699-6302
Phone: (919) 807-3304
Fax: (919) 807-3198 or (919) 807-3407
Web site: http://www.ncpublicschools.org/state_board

Exceptional Children Division
Academically/Intellectually Gifted
Web site: http://www.ncpublicschools.org/ec

North Dakota

North Dakota Department of Public Instruction
600 E. Boulevard Ave., Dept. 201
Floors 9, 10, and 11
Bismarck, ND 58505-0440
Phone: (701) 328-2260
Fax: (701) 328-2461
Web site: http://www.dpi.state.nd.us

Ohio

Ohio Association for Gifted Children (OAGC)
P.O. Box 30801
Gahanna, OH 43230
Web site: http://www.oagc.com

Ohio Department of Education
25 S. Front St.
Columbus, OH 43215-4183
Phone: (877) 644-6338
Web site: http://www.ode.state.oh.us

Office for Exceptional Children
Mike Armstrong, Director
E-mail: Mike.Armstrong@ode.state.oh.us
Web site: http://www.ode.state.oh.us/exceptional_children/
Gifted_Children

Oklahoma

Oklahoma Association for Gifted, Creative, and Talented (OAGCT)
Marti Sudduth, President
E-mail: marti-sudduth@utulsa.edu
Web site: http://www.oagct.org

Oklahoma State Department of Education
2500 N. Lincoln Blvd.
Oklahoma City, OK 73105-4599
Phone: (405) 521-3301
Fax: (405) 521-6205
Web site: http://www.sde.state.ok.us/home/defaultie.html

Gifted and Talented Office
Phone: (405) 521-4287
Web site: http://title3.sde.state.ok.us/gifted

Oregon

Oregon Association for Talented and Gifted (OATAG)
P.O. Box 1703
Beaverton, OR 97075
Web site: http://www.oatag.org

Oregon Department of Education
255 Capitol St. NE
Salem, OR 97310-0203
Phone: (503) 378-3569
Fax: (503) 378-5156
TDD: (503) 378-2892
Web site: http://www.ode.state.or.us

Gifted and Talented
Laura Pehkonen
Phone: (503) 378-3600 (ext. 2313)
E-mail: laura.pehkonen@state.or.us
Web site: http://www.ode.state.or.us/sped/spedareas/tag/tag.htm

Pennsylvania

Pennsylvania Association for Gifted Education (PAGE)
3026 Potshop Road
Norristown, PA 19403
Phone: (215) 616-0470
Web site: http://www.penngifted.org

Pennsylvania Department of Education
333 Market St.
Harrisburg, PA 17126
Phone: (717) 783-6788
Web site: http://www.pde.state.pa.us

Gifted Education
Phone: (717) 787-8913
Web site: http://www.pde.state.pa.us/gifted_ed

Rhode Island

Rhode Island Advocates for Gifted Education (RIAGE)
766 Laten Knight Road
Cranston, RI 02921
Web site: http://www.riage.org

Rhode Island Department of Elementary and Secondary Education
255 Westminster St.
Providence, RI 02903
Phone: (401) 222-4600
Web site: http://www.ridoe.net

Special Education: Talent Development
Kathy Cardoza
E-mail: ride0817@ride.ri.net
Web site: http://www.ridoe.net/Special_needs/talentdev.htm

South Carolina

South Carolina Department of Education
Rutledge Bldg.
1429 Senate St.
Columbia, SC 29201
Phone: (803) 734-8815
Fax: (803) 734-3389
Web site: http://www.sde.state.sc.us

Gifted and Talented
Wayne Lord, Education Consultant
Phone: (803) 734-8335
Fax: (803) 734-3927
E-mail: wlord@sde.state.sc.us
Web site:
http://www.myscschools.com/offices/cso/Gifted_Talented/gt.htm

South Dakota

South Dakota Association for Gifted Education
Web site: http://www.sd-agc.org

South Dakota Department of Education and Cultural Affairs
700 Governor's Dr.
Pierre, SD 57501
Web site: http://www.state.sd.us/deca

Tennessee

Tennessee Association for the Gifted (TAG)
Suzanne Terrell
1924 Belvedere Ct.
Maryville, TN 37803
E-mail: suzannet@icx.net
Web site: http://www.tag-tenn.org

Tennessee Department of Education
6th Floor, Andrew Johnson Tower
710 James Robertson Pkwy.
Nashville TN 37243-0375
Phone: (615) 741-2731
Web site: http://www.state.tn.us/education

Texas

Texas Association for the Gifted and Talented (TAGT)
Jay McIntire, Executive Director
406 E. 11th St., Ste. 310
Austin, TX 78701
Voice mail: (512) 499-8248
Fax: (512) 499-8264
E-mail: txgifted_jmcintire@yahoo.com
Web site: http://www.txgifted.org

Texas Education Agency
1701 N. Congress Ave.
Austin, TX 78701-1494
Phone: (512) 463-9734
Web site: http://www.tea.state.tx.us

Division of Advanced Academic Services
Ann Wink of Gifted Education
Phone: (512) 463-9455
Fax: (512) 305-8920
E-mail: gted@tea.state.tx.us
Web site: http://www.tea.state.tx.us/gted

Utah

Utah Association for Gifted Children (UAGC)
P.O. Box 9332
Salt Lake City, UT 84109
Web site: http://www.uagc.org

Utah State Office of Education
250 E. 500 South
P.O. Box 144200
Salt Lake City, UT 84114-4200
Phone: (801) 538-7500
Web site: http://www.usoe.k12.ut.us

Gifted and Talented
Connie Amos
Phone: (801) 538-7743
Fax: (801) 538-7769
E-mail: camos@usoe.k12.ut.us.
Web site: http://www.usoe.k12.ut.us/curr/g&t/default.htm

Vermont

Vermont Council for Gifted Education
Carol Story
Johnson State College
337 College Hill
Johnson, VT 05656
E-mail: rjensen@myrealbox.com
Web site: http://www.vcge.org

Vermont Department of Education
120 State St.
Montpelier, VT 05620
E-mail: edinfo@doe.state.vt.us
Web site: http://www.state.vt.us/educ

Virginia

Virginia Association for the Gifted
P.O. Box 26212
Richmond, VA 23260-6212
Voice mail: (804) 355-5945
Fax: (804) 355-5137
E-mail: vagifted@attbi.com
Web site: http://www.vagifted.org

Virginia Department of Education
P.O. Box 2120
Richmond, VA 23218
Phone: (800) 292-3820
Web site: http://www.pen.k12.va.us

Gifted Education
Barbara McGonagill
Voice mail: (804) 225-2884
Fax: (804) 692-3163
E-mail: bmcgonag@pen.k12.va.us
Web site: http://www.pen.k12.va.us/VDOE/Instruction/
Gifted/gifted.htm

Washington

**Washington Association of Educators
of the Talented and Gifted (WAETG)**
P.O. Box 870
Coupeville, WA 98239-0870
Phone: (360) 679-7677
E-mail: BobS@waetag.net
Web site: http://www.waetag.net

Northwest Gifted Child Association
P.O. Box 1226
Bellevue, WA 98009
Voice mail: (206) 528-9240
Voice mail: (800) 864-2073

E-mail: baesman@gte.net
Web site: http://www.innw.net/explorers/nwgca.htm

Office of Superintendent of Public Instruction (OSPI)
Old Capitol Bldg.
P.O. Box 47200
Olympia, WA 98504-7200
Phone: (360) 725-6000
TTY: (360) 664-3631
Web site: http://www.k12.wa.us

West Virginia

West Virginia Association for Gifted and Talented (WVAGT)
Janet Gould
HC-66, P.O. Box 19
Romney, WV 26757
Web site: http://www.geocities.com/wvgifted

West Virginia Department of Education
1900 Kanawha Blvd. East
Charleston, WV 25305
Web site: http://wvde.state.wv.us

Office of Special Education
Cheryl Keffer, Gifted Education
Phone: (304) 558-2696 (ext. 228)
Fax: (304) 558-3741
E-mail: ckeffer@ access.k12.wv.us
Web site: http://wvde.state.wv.us/ose/index.html

Wisconsin

Wisconsin Association for Gifted and Talented (WATG)
1608 W. Cloverdale Dr.
Appleton, WI 54914
Phone: (920) 991-9177
Fax: (920) 991-1225

E-mail: watg@focol.org
Web site: http://www.focol.org/watg

Wisconsin Department of Public Instruction
125 S. Webster St.
P.O. Box 7841
Madison, WI 53707-7841
Phone: (800) 441-4563
Web site: http://www.dpi.state.wi.us/index.html

Gifted and Talented
Mary Parks
Phone: (608) 266-3706
Fax: (608) 266-1965
E-mail: mary.parks@dpi.state.wi.us
Web site: http://www.dpi.state.wi.us/dpi/dlsis/cal/caltgts.html

Wyoming

Wyoming Association of Gifted Education (WAGE)
Marcia McChesney
28 Owl Creek Road
Sheridan, WY 82801
Phone: (307) 672-3497

Wyoming State Department of Education
2300 Capitol Ave.
Hathaway Bldg., 2nd Floor
Cheyenne, WY 82002-0050
Phone: (307) 777-7675
Fax: (307) 777-6234
Web site: http://www.k12.wy.us/index.htm

Gifted and Talented
Eve Paulson, Secretary
Phone: (307) 777-6231
E-mail: epauls@educ.state.wy.us

Canadian
National Organizations

Gifted Canada
Web site: http://www3.bc.sympatico.ca/giftedcanada/index.html

Canadian Council for Exceptional Children
Web site: http://canadian.cec.sped.org

Candadian Centers for Gifted Education

Centre for Gifted Education
University of Calgary
170 Education Block
2500 University Dr. NW
Calgary, AB, Canada, T2N 1N4
Phone: (403) 220-7799
Fax: (403) 210-2068
E-mail: gifteduc@ucalgary.ca
Web site: http://www.ucalgary.ca/~gifteduc

Canadian Associations
and Departments of Education

Alberta

Alberta Association for Bright Children (AABC/Alberta)
6240-113 St., Rm. 1280
Edmonton, AB, Canada, T6H 3L2
Phone: (780) 422-0362
Fax: (780) 413-1631
E-mail: aabc@edmc.net
Web site: http://www.freenet.edmonton.ab.ca/aabc

Alberta Learning (Alberta Government)
7th Floor, Commerce Place
10155 102 St.
Edmonton, AB, Canada, T5J 4L5
Phone: (780) 427-7219

Fax: (780) 422-1263
E-mail: comm.contact@learning.gov.ab.ca
Web site: http://www.learning.gov.ab.ca/default.asp

Special Programs Branch (Gifted and Talented)
10th Floor, East Devonian Bldg.
11160 Jasper Ave.
Edmonton, AB, Canada, T5K 0L2
Phone: (780) 422–6326
Fax: (780) 422–2039
Web site: http://www.learning.gov.ab.ca/k_12/specialneeds

British Columbia

Gifted Children's Association of British Columbia
210 W. Broadway, 3rd Floor
Vancouver, BC, Canada, V5Y 3W2
Phone: (877) 707-6111
E-mail: David_Shepherd@telus.net
Web site: http://www.gcabc.ca

British Columbia Ministry of Education
P.O. Box 9150, Stn Prov Govt
Victoria, BC, Canada, V8W 9H1
Phone: (250) 356-2500
Fax: (250) 356-5945
Web site: http://www.gov.bc.ca/bced

Gifted Education
Web site: http://www.bced.gov.bc.ca/specialed/gifted/

Manitoba

Manitoba Education and Youth
Phone: (204) 945-3744
Fax: (204) 945-4261
E-mail: mgi@gov.mb.ca
Web site: http://www.edu.gov.mb.ca/index.html

New Brunswick

The Association for Bright Children, New Brunswick Chapter
Carol Ann White, Cochair
169 Chamberlain Road
Quispamsis, NB, Canada, E2G 1B7
Phone: (506) 847-4189
Web site: http://www.sjfn.nb.ca/community_hall/A/asso4180.html

New Brunswick Department of Education
Place 2000
P.O. Box 6000
Fredericton, NB, Canada, E3B 5H1
Phone: (506) 453-3678
Fax: (506) 453-3325
Web site: http://www.gnb.ca/0000/index-e.asp

Newfoundland

Newfoundland and Labrador Association for Gifted Children (NLAGC)
David McKenzie
61 Flats Road
CBS, NL, Canada, A1W 3C5
Phone: (709) 834-4051
E-mail: nlagc@stemnet.nf.ca
Web site: http://www.stemnet.nf.ca/Community/NLAGC/nlagc.html

Newfoundland and Labrador Department of Education
P.O. Box 8700
St. John's, NL, Canada, A1B 4J6
Phone: (709) 729-5097
Fax: (709) 729-5896
E-mail: webmaster@mail.gov.nf.ca
Web site: http://www.gov.nf.ca/edu

Nova Scotia

Association for Bright Children of Nova Scotia
David W. Richey
P.O. Box 723
Dartmouth, NS, Canada, B2Y 3Z3
Phone: (902) 465-4481
Fax: (902) 463-4319
E-mail: rfurling@gcameronassoc.com
Web site: http://www.dal.ca/~stanet/database/abc.html

Nova Scotia Department of Education
P.O. Box 578
2021 Brunswick St., Ste. 402
Halifax, NS, Canada, B3J 2S9
Phone: (902) 424-5168
Fax: (902) 424-0511
Web site: http://www.ednet.ns.ca

Ontario

Ontario Association for Bright Children
P.O. Box 156, Ste. 100
2 Bloor St. West
Toronto, ON, Canada, M4W 2G7
Phone: (416) 925-6136
E-mail: abcinfo@abcontario.ca
Web site: http://www.abcontario.ca

Ontario Gifted
P.O. Box 66055
1355 Kingston Road
Pickering, ON, Canada, L1V 6P7
E-mail: ontario.gifted@sympatico.ca
Web site: http://www.ontariogifted.org

Ontario Ministry of Education
Mowat Block, 900 Bay St.
Toronto, ON, Canada M7A 1L2

Phone: (800) 387-5514
Fax: (416) 325-6348
E-mail: info@edu.gov.on.ca
Web site: http://www.edu.gov.on.ca/eng/welcome.html

Prince Edward Island

Prince Edward Island Department of Education
Second Floor, Sullivan Bldg.
16 Fitzroy St., P.O. Box 2000
Charlottetown, PE, Canada, C1A 7N8
Phone: (902) 368-4600
Fax: (902) 368-4663
Web site: http://www.edu.pe.ca

Quebec

Ministère de l'Éducation/Education Quebec
1035, Rue De La Chevrotière
QC Canada, G1R 5A5
Phone: (418) 643-7095
Fax: (418) 646-6561
E-mail: cim.rens@meq.gouv.qc.ca
Web site: http://www.meq.gouv.qc.ca/GR-PUB/m_englis.htm

Saskatchewan

Saskatchewan Learning
2200 College Ave.
Regina, SK, Canada, S4P 3V7
Web site: http://www.sasked.gov.sk.ca

Saskatchewan Teachers' Federation
2317 Arlington Ave.
Saskatoon, SK, Canada, S7J 2H8
Toll-free: (800) 667-7762
Fax: (306) 374-1122
E-mail: stf@stf.sk.ca
Web site: http://www.stf.sk.ca/index.htm

Gifted Resources
Web site: http://www.stf.sk.ca/src/prof_res_serv/bibliog/gifted.htm

Northwest Territories

Government of the Northwest Territories: Education, Culture, and Employment
P.O. Box 1320
Yellowknife, NT, Canada, X1A 2L9
Phone: (867) 669-2366
Fax: (867) 873-0169
Web site: http://siksik.learnnet.nt.ca/index.html

Nunavik

Nunavik Department of Education
Iqaluit, NU Canada
Phone: (888) 531-1456
Fax: (867) 975-5605
Web site: http://www.gov.nu.ca/Nunavut/English/phone/
education.shtml

Yukon

Government of Yukon: Department of Education
P.O. Box 2703
Whitehorse, YK, Canada, Y1A 2C6
Phone: (867) 667-5141
Fax: (867) 393-6254
E-mail: contact.education@gov.yk.ca
Web site: http://www.gov.yk.ca/depts/education/index.html